John D. Rockefeller

Anointed with Oil

John D. Rockefeller

Anointed with Oil

Grant Segall

Dedicated to my writing coach and beloved wife, Victoria Belfiglio

OXFORD
UNIVERSITY PRESS

Oxford New York
Athens Auckland Bangkok Bogotá Buenos Aires Calcutta
Cape Town Chennai Dar es Salaam Delhi Florence Hong Kong Istanbul
Karachi Kuala Lumpur Madrid Melbourne Mexico City Mumbai
Nairobi Paris São Paulo Singapore Taipei Tokyo Toronto Warsaw
and associated companies in
Berlin Ibadan

Published by Oxford University Press, Inc.
198 Madison Avenue, New York, New York 10016
www.oup.com

Design: Greg Wozney
Layout: Alexis Siroc
Picture research: Fran Antmann

Library of Congress Cataloging-in-Publication Data
Segall, Grant.
John D. Rockefeller / Grant Segall.
p. cm. - (Oxford portraits)
Includes bibliographical references and index.
ISBN 0-19-512147-3
1. Rockefeller, John D. (John Davison), 1839-1937-Juvenile literature. 2. Businessmen-United States-Biography-Juvenile literature. 3. Capitalists and financiers-United States-Biography-Juvenile literature. 4. Industrialists-United States-Biography-Juvenile literature. 5. Philanthropists-United States-Biography-Juvenile literature. 6. Standard Oil Company-History-Juvenile literature. [1. Rockefeller, John D. (John Davison), 1839-1937. 2. Capitalists and financiers. 3. Millionaires. 4. Philanthropists.] I. Title. II. Series.
HC102.5.R548 S44 2000
338.7'6223382'092-dc21
[B] 00-044616

9 8 7 6 5 4 3 2 1

Printed in the United States of America
on acid-free paper

On the cover: John D. Rockefeller in 1880.
Frontispiece: The busy Rockefeller takes time to pose in his mid-40s.

Contents

I believe the power of making money is a gift of God. . . . I believe it is my duty to go on making money and still more money, and to dispose of the money I make for the good of my fellow man according to the dictates of my conscience.

—John D. Rockefeller,
interviewed by reporter William Hoster in 1906

A young Rockefeller (right) poses with his siblings Will and Mary Ann. Speaking years later about his youth, he would say, "I was much more dignified than I am now. I was very sedate and earnest, preparing to meet the responsibilities of life."

CHAPTER

The First Foothold

It was springtime in the mid-1840s, and the turkey hens were sneaking into the brush again on John D. Rockefeller's childhood farm. "I can still close my eyes," he would write in his memoirs decades later, "and distinctly see the gentle and dignified birds walking quietly along the brook and through the woods, cautiously stealing the way to their nests." Perhaps it took one to know one. The gentle and dignified John stole quietly and cautiously after a hen across the field. She noticed him, zigzagged awhile, then vanished into the brush. John, age seven or eight, stalked her again the next day. She vanished again. But the persistent hen had met her match. He eventually found her nest.

That was the beginning of John's first business venture. His mother had said he could raise the hen's babies and sell them. One by one, he slipped the eggs from the nest and put them in the barn, safe from the rats and foxes outside. Then he brought the hen inside to sit on them. When the eggs hatched, he tended the babies with care. He fed them curds, bread crumbs, and grasshoppers. He guarded them on walks. But he had no qualms about selling them in the fall. With the profits, he bought three more hens the next spring. The profits grew. "I can still see, upon the mantel," he would tell his biographer, "the little box with the lattice top that I kept my money in, silver and gold."

John loved the money and more. As an American, he wanted to help his young nation prosper. As a Baptist, he wanted to fulfill the Protestant work ethic by making the most of God's gifts. "Accomplishment!" he would say. "That is the goal of every man who tries to do his part in the world."

During his 97 years, John D. Rockefeller built the world's biggest financial nest egg and played one of the world's biggest parts. As the world's leading oilman he pioneered many features of modern business, from global monopolies to management committees. He became one of the world's most hated people, too, his name a synonym, fairly or not, for ruthless greed. But he also became the world's biggest backer of charities. He helped to promote many of their modern features, from global foundations to matching grants. And he founded one of the world's foremost families, a family that has led business, philanthropy, government, and the arts for more than a century.

Rockefeller was secretive and mystifying. He wore paper vests but sported monogrammed onyx cufflinks. He reused packing paper yet owned four homes, one on nearly five square miles of ground. He kept his word and his faith with care, but his businesses crushed rivals and broke laws. Through it all, he had an air of patient kindness that could be more maddening than naked greed. "Jawn D.," wrote slang humorist Finley Peter Dunne, "hasn't anny idee that he iver done wrong to annywan."

Rockefeller came from a family on the move. One branch had fled persecution of Protestants in France, then sailed from Germany to America. Other branches had sailed from England and Scotland. Rockefeller's paternal grandfather, Godfrey, kept seeking greener farms for himself, his wife, and the nine survivors among their ten children. After

John D. Rockefeller's father was the handsome, reckless William Avery Rockefeller. A neighbor called Big Bill "the best-dressed man for miles around."

trying five farms in the East, Godfrey yearned for the wilds of Michigan. But his wife, Lucy, balked. The former teacher, descended from a British king, was taller, better educated, more diligent, and braver than Godfrey. She once tore a patch from a burglar's coat as he fled her house and shamed him a few days later by sewing it back in front of his friends. She agreed to move west only halfway across the southern tier of New York, to the outskirts of Richford, a hamlet near some relatives. The family found a knoll with a pretty view of forests and streams below—the sort of view that John D. Rockefeller would seek in his country estates.

Godfrey and Lucy's third child, William Avery Rockefeller, became known as "Big Bill" or "Devil Bill." He was a striking man: broad, strong, and swift, almost six

Rockefeller's cautious mother, Eliza Davison Rockefeller, took only one known gamble in her life: She married Big Bill.

feet tall, with blue eyes, a quick smile, a firm jaw, and a fierce will. He built a small clapboard cottage near his parents and flustered the neighbors by taking in a poor, pretty woman, Nancy Brown, supposedly as a housekeeper.

Big Bill hated tobacco and liquor but spent hours in taverns, swapping yarns and hinting at secret ways of making money. In truth, he roamed the countryside buying and selling whatever he could: salt, lumber, furs, horses, and what passed for medicines in those unregulated days. "Dr. William A. Rockefeller, the Celebrated Cancer Specialist," his handbills said. At least one of his medicines contained the liquor he loathed and the oil his son would refine.

Local lore holds that Big Bill softened up many customers by pretending to be deaf and dumb. At about age 26, he supposedly played the trick some 30 miles north of Richford, at the home of John Davison, a prosperous farmer and stern Baptist. Davison must have been leery of Bill. His wife had died after taking a peddler's pill. But Bill intrigued the farmer's youngest daughter, Eliza. She could have been Lucy Rockefeller's daughter, for she had Lucy's blue eyes, strong chin, industry, and pluck. From a sickbed, Eliza once scared away a burglar by singing a hymn. She smoked a corncob pipe, to Bill's regret, but shared his scorn for liquor. She also had red hair, a narrow waist, and a witty tongue. At about 23, she was an old maid by the era's standards. She made what seemed like a safe joke about Bill: "I'd marry that man if he were not deaf and dumb." He spoke up, and before long she kept her word, apparently without her father's consent.

Soon this unlikely couple was living in Bill's cottage with Nancy Brown. We can only guess Eliza's suspicions about her, but the women seemed to get along, even during Bill's absences that lasted for months. They had their first two babies about the same time as each other. But, at the Davisons' insistence, Bill finally sent Nancy away, too soon for the two sets of children to remember each other.

The Rockefellers named their first child Lucy, for Bill's mother. Seventeen months later, on the night of July 8, 1839, Eliza went into labor again in the parents' small bedroom. A neighboring woman heated water and prepared bandages. The baby came fast, just before midnight.

He was named John Davison for Eliza's father. The child was always called John, never Johnny or Jack. He grew to walk slowly, pensively, with stooped shoulders. He had a slim body and a grave face, slightly pinched in the middle. He had a wide mouth, thin lips, and hooded bluish eyes. He often gazed inwardly one moment, then seemed to stare through an onlooker's skin the next.

John liked to play with other children, especially if they let him choose the game. If not, he was happy to keep score for them, cutting notches on a stick. He loved to calculate, no matter how long it took. He told a restless opponent at checkers, "I'll move just as soon as I get it figured out." He had the perfect temperament for such battles of wit: patient and aggressive by just the right turns, creative in his means, relentless in his ends.

He also had a subtle humor, sometimes to his growing family's regret. He often teased the third child, William, with a straight face. He once spun the sled of the fourth child, Mary Ann, into a ditch and made a deadpan apology. He perched himself and his book atop a pole during an outdoor study period at school, until Eliza came by and ordered him down.

Eliza ruled her brood with switches from trees when necessary. John once secretly slashed a switch with a knife, to soften its blows. It broke against his back. She told him to fetch another and be sure not to slash it this time. He and Will slipped out to skate one night and rescued a drowning neighbor. Eliza praised them for the rescue and whipped them for the infraction. John once convinced her of his innocence in mid-whipping. "Never mind," she said, "we have started in on this whipping, and it will do for the next time."

Eliza hated to waste anything, even a whipping. "Willful waste makes woeful want," she used to say. She had to stretch her money during her husband's absences. She ran up a debt at a general store of nearly $1,000—about $17,500 today.

Bill usually brought back fancy clothes, fancy horses, wads of cash, and a handful of coins for the children. But he sometimes left them wanting. "My father promised me a Shetland pony near 60 years ago and I never got the pony," John would write decades later, in a rare complaint, while apologizing for food that had disappointed poor children at his estate's yearly picnic.

Bill sometimes taught hard lessons. When John was a toddler, his father held out his arms to catch him, then let him fall to the floor. "Never trust anyone completely, not even me," Bill said.

The Rockefellers made the first of many moves when John was about four. They went to the outskirts of Moravia, New York, a village near Eliza's father. They bought a house of five rooms and added two or three more. It stood on 92 acres atop another scenic hill, this one overlooking Lake Owasco, one of the Finger Lakes. The region was simmering with ideas. Native son Millard Fillmore, soon to be President, was championing railways and other aids to business. Religious reformers were fighting liquor and slavery. Early feminists held a historic woman's rights convention in nearby Seneca Falls when John was nine.

By then, the boy had many chores, from pulling weeds to milking the cow. According to a neighbor, Eliza used to call up to John's attic bedroom before dawn and say, "If you don't wake up and set to work with a will, you'll find yourself in the county [poor] house." The truth was, he shared his parents' strong wills and Eliza's scorn for waste, especially of effort. He earned money from extra chores, such as raising his turkeys on their farm and digging a neighbor's potatoes for 37 1/2 cents a day. But he also found ways to make more money for less work. He bought candy by the pound and sold it to his brothers and sisters by the piece. He loaned a neighbor $50 and made $3.50 in interest over six months. "The impression was gaining ground with me," he would tell a men's group decades later, "that it was a good thing to let the money be my servant and not make myself a slave to the money." His mastery amazed his siblings. "When it's raining porridge," Lucy would reportedly say, "you'll find John's dish right side up."

His father taught him to "trade dishes for platters"—that is, to get the better part of any deal. "I cheat my boys every chance I get," Big Bill once bragged. "I want to make 'em sharp." But he also taught them to pay debts and honor contracts. And he whetted John's hunger for wealth by taking him on a business trip to bustling Syracuse and buying him gleaming leather shoes there. A grown John would call cities sinful, but he would help to make them capitals of nationwide industries and turn America from heavily rural to mostly urban during his lifetime.

Bill was a good husband and father at times. While the family sang along, he often played the melodeon—a small reed organ—or the violin, holding it at his waist, country style. He taught his three sons to drive horses, shoot rifles, and swim. He stocked the lake with pickerel and taught them to catch the fish. He urged them not to smoke or drink—pleas eventually rejected by his younger boys but never by John. He called for a neighborhood school and collected the taxes for it with few arguments.

The one-room schoolhouse was open for just a few months each year, but John made the most of them. He questioned his teachers long and hard. He double-checked their answers. He carried his slate against his chest like a treasure. Bill had no use for the occasional church services held at school, but Eliza always took the children and had them put some of their hard-earned money into the collection plate.

The family's life became harder in Moravia. Bill's income grew shakier and his absences longer. John did his best to replace him. He helped keep the family accounts and became a second father to the siblings who followed him every two years or so: the outgoing Will, the sharp-tongued Mary Ann, and the fraternal twins, headstrong Franklin and sickly Francis (a girl, despite the name's spelling), who died before turning two.

Rumors arose that their father was womanizing and trading stolen horses. When John was 10, a court ordered Bill to repay Eliza's father a debt of about $1,200. Worse yet, Bill was indicted for raping a female servant, but he was

never tried. John would never say what, if anything, he knew about these scandals. But they may have reinforced two of his biggest strengths and limitations: his scorn for criticism and his penchant for privacy.

The Old Academy at Owego trained not just John D. Rockefeller but a staunch ally of big business, Republican leader Thomas C. Platt, and a staunch foe of Rockefeller's, Congregational minister Washington Gladden, who dubbed the oilman's donations "tainted money."

Soon the Rockefellers fled to the outskirts of Owego, some 18 miles south of Richford. Owego was a county seat with more than 7,000 people. The family rented two houses in turn, both with views of the Susquehanna River. John took a paternal liking to a little girl who lived nearby. When she died, he lay grieving in her yard all day.

He attended a Baptist church and Sunday school in downtown Owego. He also went to a neighborhood school for two years, then the downtown Owego Academy for one year. The big, brick, prestigious academy charged $3 to $5 per course. He liked its scientific equipment, which included a generator, telegraph, and skeleton. He also liked its lessons in mental arithmetic. Years later, in buying a million-dollar pipeline, he encouraged the seller to chat for half an hour while Rockefeller thought out a payment plan that saved him $30,000. But he felt awkward downtown in his homespun clothes. He was left out of a class photograph on their account. He reportedly vowed to a friend to be able to afford them and more someday: "I want to be worth $100,000. And I'm going to be, too."

Early in 1853, the Rockefellers moved again, this time some 300 miles west to Cleveland, Ohio, a boomtown of 26,000 people. It overlooked Lake Erie and the Cuyahoga River, which Rockefeller's oil business would help to pollute not many years later. It stood at the tip of the Ohio & Erie Canal, which linked the Great Lakes with the Gulf of Mexico, and a new railroad line, which would make the canal obsolete but the city more important than ever. It lay in another reform-minded region, with its own woman's rights conventions. It also bordered America's vast plains, a fresh sales territory for Big Bill.

For a few years, most of the Rockefellers shuttled between the city and the outskirts. John and Will stayed with a landlady downtown in their family's absence, but often visited their parents in the country. John courted their teenage servant until her parents rescued her, hoping for a son-in-law with a better future than this quiet bumpkin seemed to have.

Perhaps in anger or shame at his rambling father, John told a school principal that his mother was a widow. The boy was assigned first to grammar school, then to Cleveland's new Central High School, launched reportedly as the westernmost of the nation's free public high schools. Central taught everything from astronomy to economics to surveying. John did not learn to be a sure speller or a deep reader, preferring his occasional books to be light and inspirational. But he grew to write and speak as clearly and earnestly as he thought. He gained a lifelong nickname, John D., by putting his middle initial on his papers. He also gained a brief nickname, "Old Pleased-Although-I'm Sad," by describing himself that way in a class speech. "He was soberly mirthful," classmate Lucy Spelman would say. He seldom laughed, but often smiled to himself.

Playing outside one day, John kicked a ball that nearly knocked a painter off a ladder. The boy tried vainly to placate the angry man. Then a wealthy classmate named Marcus Alonzo Hanna came to his rescue and beat the painter up. Hanna would later fight for John and other business leaders as a powerful United States senator.

Inside the classroom, on the girls' side of the aisle, sat Lucy Maria (Lute) and Laura Celestia (Cettie) Spelman. Lute, two years older, was the adopted daughter of a former state representative and his wife. Laura, their natural daughter, could have been a Rockefeller. Two months younger than John, she had the Rockefellers' firm chin, arched eyebrows, and sparkling eyes (although dark brown, not the Rockefeller blue). She had a hint of Eliza's red hair. She was the rare girl of her day to study that favorite Rockefeller subject, business. She sang, played the piano, and shunned liquor for life. Her Congregational family was as pious as most of the Rockefellers, cooking on Sundays only when hosting slaves fleeing to nearby Canada on what was called the Underground Railroad. Above all, she had the Rockefeller pluck. "Women, even as man, can 'paddle her own canoe,'" she declared in a bold graduation speech for her day. John did not court Laura during their school days. "My mind was on other things just then," he would explain. But he made note of her for the future.

In the pride of old age, Rockefeller would claim to have studied voice and piano six hours a day during his youth. But it is hard to imagine him spending so much time for so little financial or spiritual gain. He was surely too busy with his studies at Central High School and activities at the young Erie Street Baptist Church. He and other members ushered during services, swept floors, washed windows, and lit lamps. They also attended two services on Sundays, several prayer meetings a week, and the church's occasional parties and picnics. At 15, John was baptized and put in charge of a Bible class. He also used his rich baritone voice to sing in the choir.

Tall and lanky, with sandy-colored hair, John dreamed of becoming the first Rockefeller to attend college. Eliza encouraged a broad education, but Big Bill, about to incur hidden expenses, told him to do something more practical. So the boy quit Central about two months before graduation and spent three months at a more specialized college than he'd had in mind: a commercial college about to merge with the flagship of the Bryant and Stratton business schools. These schools would sweep the country soon, and so would their flowery Spencerian penmanship, a style of script surviving today on cans of Classic Coca-Cola. For a onetime fee of $40, students also studied bookkeeping, banking, business ethics, and more.

In August came perhaps the hardest task of John's young life: finding work. The 16-year-old tramped Cleveland's hot streets all day, six days a week, with vague but strong dreams. "I did not guess what it would be, but I was after something big," he would tell his biographer. Jobs happened to be tight then, however. He tried the same employers two and three times each. "It's all right, John," Bill said on September 25. "You go out to the country, and I'll take care of you." Years later, Rockefeller would say the offer still sent "a cold chill" down his spine. "What would have become of me if I had gone to the country?"

The next day, autumn was in the air. John went out that morning with "desperate determination." After more rejections, he tried Hewitt and Tuttle, a general wholesale firm in a three-story brick building a block from the Cuyahoga. Henry Tuttle spoke with him for a few minutes and invited him to return that afternoon. John walked around the corner, then broke into a skip of delight. In the afternoon, he showed his handwriting to Isaac Hewitt. "We will give you a chance," said Hewitt. John put on sleeve guards and mounted a stool that felt like a throne. "That was a momentous day to me," he would say, "getting the first foothold, the chance to earn my living." He would celebrate September 26 as "Job Day," hosting a small party and hoisting the American flag.

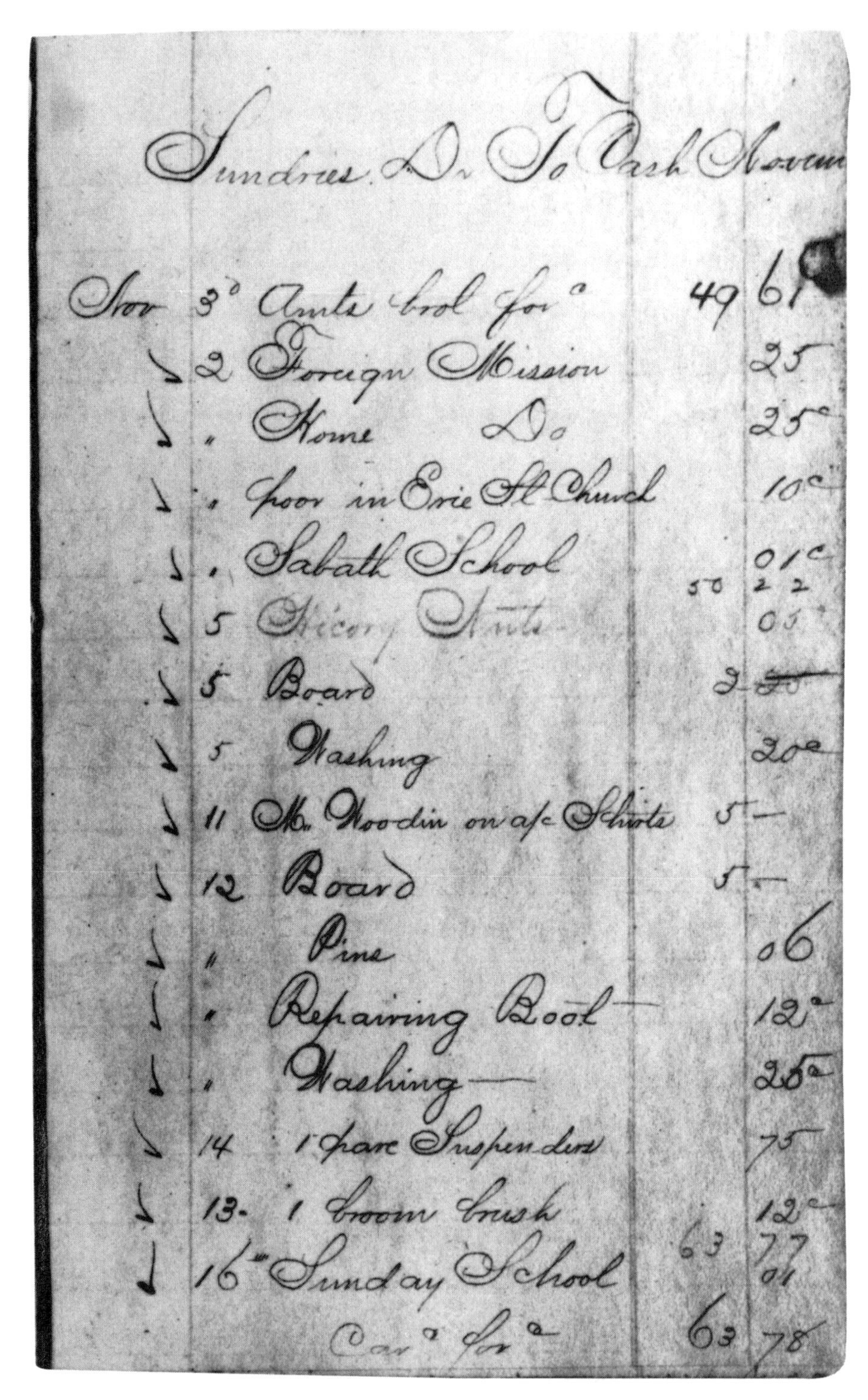

Sundries Dr To Cash Movem

Nov	3d	Amts brot ford	49	61
	2	Foreign Mission		25
	"	Home Do		25
	"	Poor in Erie St Church		10
	"	Sabath School		01
			50	22
	5	Hickory Nuts		05
	5	Board	2	50
	5	Washing		20
	11	Mr Woodin on a/c Shirts	5	—
	12	Board	5	—
	"	Pins		06
	"	Repairing Boot		12
	"	Washing		25
	14	1 pair Suspenders		75
	13	1 broom brush		12
			63	77
	16th	Sunday School		01
		Card ford	63	78

John D. Rockefeller was a meticulous accountant, noting every penny earned or spent in a notebook he called Ledger A.

CHAPTER

2

The Oil Business Head and Ears

Rockefeller's bosses said nothing about pay at first. He did not complain. He was happy just to learn about business. Hewitt and Tuttle helped to link an increasingly national economy. They handled shipments by wagon, train, or boat of everything from grain to marble. Rockefeller inspected deliveries, corrected bills, paid them, and recorded the payments in the firm's books. "This was so delightful to me, all the method and system of the office," he would write. He served the system faithfully. He refused a boatman's demands to pad an invoice. He pressed a debtor quietly but steadily for an hour. The man finally gave in, saying, "I never saw such a pestering collector!"

After some three months, about New Year's Day, Hewitt finally gave Rockefeller $50 and a salary of $25 a month (about $454 a month in modern dollar values, far below minimum wage). "I felt like a criminal," Rockefeller would recall. He strove to deserve the money. He came at 6:30 a.m. He ate a lunch from home at his desk. He often returned after supper. He once tried to slow down. "I have this day covenanted with myself not to be seen after 10 o'clock p.m." At work, he wrote in a dime notebook that he labeled Ledger A. But he soon gave up, adding, "Don't make any more such covenants." Years later, he would still have nightmares about the job and wake up crying, "I can't collect So-and-So's account!" But he also had daydreams of wealth. He once peeked longingly at a banknote for $4,000 in the office safe. "It seemed like an awfully large sum to me, an unheard-of amount," he would tell friends years later.

Ledger A was the first of a lifelong series of scrupulous account books. It shows great thrift: 3 cents for apples, 13 for a shirt collar, 88 for a gallon of lamp oil. It also shows great charity, even before his first wages. At Erie Street Church, he gave money to support preachers, poor congregants, missionaries, and a school for the poor. His gifts rose from about 6 percent of his pay the first year to 10 percent four years later. "It has seemed as if I was favored and got increases," he would tell his biographer, "because the Lord knew that I was going to turn around and give it back."

He defied the era's bitter divisions, giving to Methodist, Catholic, Jewish, and African-American causes. He helped to buy two slaves' freedom. "It is a violation of the laws of our country and the laws of God that man should hold his fellow man in bondage," he had written at Central High. He attended abolition meetings and became a lifelong member of the new Republican Party, which sought to limit slavery and promote business development. He cast his first Presidential vote for Abraham Lincoln.

Rockefeller also helped his family. He gave his siblings presents and loans. He managed his mother's inheritance from her late father. He supervised construction of a family house downtown. He got bids from eight contractors and bargained so hard that the winner lost money. Still, Big Bill charged his son rent to live there.

In 1857, Tuttle quit, and Rockefeller became Hewitt's chief aide. He also made money on the side wholesaling pork, flour, and ham. His yearly pay rose to $700 by 1859, but he felt he deserved more and a friend, Maurice Clark, agreed. A burly Englishman who liked to smoke, drink, and swear, Clark, 28, was an odd match for Rockefeller, 19. But he knew Rockefeller from business school and must have hit it off with him at first. Clark proposed that they start their own commission house for $2,000 apiece. Rockefeller had only saved only about $800, so he borrowed the rest from his father. All his life, he would nurse pennies and borrow millions for the same reason: to make them grow. He would repay every debt on time.

"Clark and Rockefeller," said a new sign on a waterfront warehouse in March 1859. "It was a great thing to be my own employer," Rockefeller would write in his memoirs. "Mentally I swelled with pride—a partner in a firm with $4,000 capital!" He prayed for humility. "Look out, or you will lose your head—go steady." He went steady, indeed. He would never have a losing year in business.

Clark and Rockefeller sought to trade meat, grain, fish, plaster, and more. Soon a late frost damaged crops. The partners spent hours culling ruined beans from a heap in the warehouse. Rockefeller mostly ran the office, but spent a few weeks courting suppliers in rural Ohio and Indiana. He won so many that he needed more loans to buy their supplies. The first banker rebuffed him. "Someday," Rockefeller shot back, "I'll be the richest man in the world." The second banker lent him $2,000. "My elation can hardly be imagined," Rockefeller would write. "I felt that I was now a man of importance." Years later, he would gratefully lend the banker money to buy Standard Oil stock.

Rockefeller borrowed more money from his father as well. But Big Bill often tested him by demanding repayment at tough moments. "He would never know how angry I felt beneath the surface," Rockefeller would tell his biographer. Still, the boy always managed to comply.

The partners once risked all the firm's money on a boatload of grain. A violent storm arose. They quickly spent $150 to insure the shipment. The storm blew over harmlessly. Rockefeller went home ill—whether over the risk they had taken or the cost of the insurance, he did not say.

The firm made $4,400 in profits the first year and $17,000 the second. Soon it sprawled across four addresses. But the partners clashed. Clark criticized both Rockefeller's gambles and his precautions, such as refusing to pay suppliers in advance. In turn, Rockefeller chided a new partner, George Gardner, for an indulgence that might scare off bankers: buying a share of a yacht and sailing on a Saturday afternoon instead of working. Gardner soon quit the firm, but would later prove diligent enough to become Cleveland's mayor.

Rockefeller made the milder indulgence of buying a horse. He also went to lectures, concerts, and meetings of the new Young Men's Christian Association. But his main social life was at church. He became a clerk, trustee, and Sunday-school teacher. In his ledger, he noted expenses for the church and added, "Let it go." Decades later, he would tease the congregation about the expenses and add, "I forgive you the debt."

The young church had bigger debts. One Sunday, Rockefeller stood on the doorstep and begged fellow members to help pay them off. He and Will also threw pebbles at a creditor's window one night, woke him up, won an extension of the debt, and helped the church raise the money to meet it. "I hope the members of the mother church were properly humiliated to see how far we had gone beyond their expectations," Rockefeller, competitive even in religion, would write about an older Baptist church in town. Echoing Laura Spelman's words, he would add, "We could paddle our own canoe."

Rockefeller was still in touch with Laura, now a teacher and assistant principal at a Cleveland elementary school. One of her pupils, a former slave named John Green, would

Laura Celestia Spelman Rockefeller was even warier of vice than her husband was. When John hosted a dance for their son, she stayed away, claiming a sudden headache but probably shunning what she considered a sinful spectacle.

become Ohio's first black state senator, tour Europe at Rockefeller's expense, and ironically help to found a holiday his patron refused to honor: Labor Day. In an 1860 letter, Laura wrote that Rockefeller "was in no particular rush to have me get married, but he hoped that in the multitude of my thoughts I would not forget the subject." He began to court her two years later, perhaps finally confident that he could support her. He brought her bouquets. He played duets with her on the Spelmans' piano. He took her to services at Erie Street Church. He gave her carriage rides. The secretive man even confided business details to her. "Her judgment was always better than mine," he would say years later. "Without her keen advice, I would be a poor man."

By then, the Civil War was raging. Frank Rockefeller enlisted and was wounded twice; his brothers, Will and John, stayed home. "I wanted to go in the army and do my part," John said later. But "we were in a new business, and if I had not stayed it must have stopped." He hired substitute soldiers to serve in his place, as did many other prosperous Northerners, and gave money to the Union cause. He also profited from the war, which boosted prices and cut off Southern competitors.

Meanwhile, another war of sorts was raging, over oil. "Black gold" or "golden grease," it was called. For centuries, people had skimmed oil from creeks or distilled it from animals and plants for use in many things, from war paints to medicinal potions like Big Bill's. They had recently learned to refine it for kerosene, a bright-burning, cheap fuel for lamps that defied the night. In 1859 they learned to drill for it, starting to sink rich wells near filmy Oil Creek in northwestern Pennsylvania, about 100 miles from Cleveland. Critics said the buried oil was the fuel of hell. But Rockefeller would tell his biographer, "These vast stores of wealth were the gifts of the great Creator."

An oil rush arose to rival the gold rush of 1849. Bars and brothels sprang up, making the Oil Regions seem as sinful as the Bible's Sodom and Gomorrah. Leaks, spills, and fumes gave the Regions the nickname of "Sodden Gomorrah." But pollution did not worry people as much then as today. They figured there was always a cleaner frontier down the trail.

An early Standard Oil Co. lamp survives at the Museum of American Financial History. Standard turned out not just kerosene and other oil products but lamps and stoves in which to burn them.

Rockefeller visited the Oil Regions in the early 1860s. He

tried to cross an oozy pit on a log. He slipped. "You have got me into the oil business head and ears," he told his host.

He saw less promise in the unpredictable wells than in the belching refineries that were springing up across the country, fouling neighbors' milk. Cleveland had 20 refineries already, linked by rail to the Regions and many big markets. In 1863, Rockefeller helped to form an $8,000 refining firm, Andrews, Clark, and Company, "thinking that this was a little side issue," as he would tell his biographer. His partners were the brothers Maurice, James, and Richard Clark, along with Samuel Andrews, a British friend of theirs who attended Erie Street Church. They opened the Excelsior Oil Works, whose name meant "upward." The works were a few stills, furnaces, and sheds

Rockefeller, toward the right, wearing a wide, light-colored hat, disapproved of the sometimes crude morals prevailing near Oil Creek in northwestern Pennsylvania. But he saw God's blessings in the region's crude oil.

on three sloping acres of red clay outside Cleveland, along the Cuyahoga River and a forthcoming railway.

Andrews, a self-taught chemist, strained the oil, boiled it, condensed it, then cleansed it with water, caustic soda, and sulfuric acid to separate the kerosene. Rockefeller helped the company's crews sweep up shavings and load barrels onto trains. As always, he fought waste both by scrimping and spending. In the opposite of today's trend of "outsourcing"—buying supplies and services from outsiders—he put plumbers, barrel makers, and other specialists on staff. He bought forests of white oak for the barrels. He fueled his furnaces with gasoline, then an unwanted by-product that rivals dumped in the river. He dealt with oil day and night. He often hosted his partners at breakfast and walked to work with them, talking oil all the way. He visited Laura after work in oil-stained boots. He woke a grumbling Will in their bedroom at night and whispered ideas.

John and Laura finally became engaged in March 1864. He bought her a diamond engagement ring for $118 (about $1,230 today). On September 8, he treated 26 workers to lunch without saying why. Then he went to Laura's home and married her. Their ministers presided, only their families attended, and whether Big Bill was present no one knows. The bride and groom were old for their day. John was 25, and Laura caught up to him the next day.

The couple honeymooned for a month. Rockefeller caught his first glimpse of Niagara Falls, Quebec, New York City, and more. He peppered the locals with questions, so distracting a guide that their buggy drifted into a ditch. John was having so much fun, he failed to itemize some expenses in his ledger, summarizing them instead as "Wedding tour, $490."

Their first Sunday back in Cleveland, the Rockefellers prayed at Erie Street, now Laura's church, too. On Monday, John went to work. On Tuesday, he went to Chicago on business. He made many such trips over the years but sent home countless letters and telegrams with a warmth that belied his grave air. "What a blessing that I have such a good & true wife.... How much I would give for wings to reach you tonight.... I dreamed last night of the girl Celestia Spelman and awoke to realize she was my Laura."

The couple stayed with Rockefeller's family at first, then rented a brick house a door or two away. Married women could not teach public school, but, without modern appliances, it was full-time work for Laura to run a home, even after hiring servants a couple of years later. The Rockefellers also toiled for religious and civic groups, and John joined business boards as well. But he thought the meetings were wastes of time. A bank board dismissed him for poor attendance. He further considered plays and dances immoral and parties and clubs unnecessary. "I was happy in my home life," he would tell his biographer.

At work, he faced rising friction. Maurice Clark complained about business debts that were nearing $100,000. James once cursed loudly and long at Rockefeller. But Big Bill was not the only member of his family who could play deaf. His son waited out the rant with his feet propped up. "Now, James," he finally said, "you can knock my head off but you might as well understand that you can't scare me."

The Clarks tried to cow him by threatening to break up the firm. Andrews secretly promised to stay with him if that happened. Rockefeller proposed new debts. The Clarks renewed their threat. He asked each partner one by one if he really meant it. Each said yes. Rockefeller immediately went to a newspaper office and announced the breakup. Maurice rushed to John's home the next morning.

"What do you mean by doing such a thing?" he demanded.

"Why, you all voted for it," Rockefeller replied.

"You really want to break up?"

"I really want to break up."

The partners got divorced on Valentine's Day, 1865. They held an auction, with the winner to get the refinery; the loser, the commission house. They quickly outbid both the refinery's apparent worth and Rockefeller's arranged loans. He kept bidding higher, anyway. Clark finally reached $72,000. Rockefeller bid $72,500, or about $772,000 today. "I'll go no higher, John," said Clark. "The business is yours."

Rockefeller would later tell his biographer, "It was the day that determined my career." He raised the extra money and renamed the firm Rockefeller and Andrews. He opened offices in both downtown Cleveland and the Oil Regions. He took in his brother Will, who combined much of John's drive with Big Bill's girth and salesmanship. Will opened a second refinery, the Standard Works, named to promise good, steady oil. Then he opened an office in Manhattan, where he wooed the nation's biggest banks and managed the firm's share of the nation's growing field of exports.

Rockefeller's new company had just started when the Civil War came to an end with the final surrender of the South in May 1865. The economy began to soar. It was the eve of what Mark Twain in 1873 would call the Gilded Age. Tycoons called "robber barons" used their profits to live high, loose lives, arousing wrath and envy. But Rockefeller poured his rising profits back into oil. Thanks to big loans, big storage tanks, and countless telegrams, he learned about price changes quickly and bought or sold accordingly. His firm grew twice as big as any rival's in Cleveland. In 1865, he refined $1.2 million worth of oil, or up to 500 42-gallon barrels of crude a day.

The brothers often communicated in code, John sometimes using the apt aliases of "Murky" or "Murkily." He tried to absorb every fact and leak none. "Success comes from keeping the ears open and the mouth closed," he liked to say. Still, as his success grew, he could not help breaking

THANKFUL, THANKFUL, THANKFUL

John D. Rockefeller showered his wife, Laura, with letters from the road. He seemed to write on whatever came to hand, from embossed stationery to the backs of telegram blanks. At age 28, he dashed off the following letter after the crash of a train the family had planned to take to New York for Christmas.

Dec 20th 1867

My Dear Wife

I arrived last eve at four O'C and after doing some Shopping to replace my Stock Clothing and Toilet articles, called on Will & Mira & spent the night very pleasantly. The Christmas presents were burned with the Valice [sic] and Umbrella, Our friends appreciate them as though rec'd and join in expressions of *gratitude* that I did not *remain* in the car with the Baggage, I do (and did when I learned that the first train left) regard the thing as the *Providence of God.* I will not by letter, rehe[a]rse particulars of the Accident, but hope to Vivavoce [orally], as early as Wednesday next. Your folks all well, I expect to spend the night with them, You no doubt rec'd my telegram sent at 6 P.M. 18th from Ongola. I[t] was *well* that a good work kept you and Bessie at home We certainly should have been in the burned car as it was the only one that went that we could have entered at the time we would have arrived at the Station—I am thankful, thankful, thankful.

Kiss the darling Baby.

Truly, Jno

The Market dull & declining
Our Money matters easy & comfortable
Can't tell about our Canal matters

into dance steps at times or chortling, "I'm bound to be rich! Bound to be rich! Bound to be rich!"

After two years of marriage, Laura gave birth to Elizabeth, apparently named for John's mother, Eliza, but always called Bessie. Cleveland's first woman doctor delivered the baby. When home, John helped to take care of Bessie, carrying her back and forth, calming her tears. The household also grew from the nearly full-time addition of Laura's sister Lute. John sometimes mimicked Lute's genteel way of lifting her skirts, but the in-laws got along well. Lute, never marrying, would live in the Rockefellers' homes for the rest of her life.

When he traveled, Rockefeller seemed to pack luck. One Sunday, oilmen tried to save their moored barrels from breaking loose in the surging waters of Oil Creek. Rockefeller prayed at a local church instead. His barrels were the only ones that survived. He once planned to take Laura and Bessie to New York and sent the family's luggage ahead to the train. Then a sudden obligation kept the mother and baby home. John dashed to the station alone, missed the train, and took the next one. The first one

Rockefeller had many partners and outposts over the years. By the late 1860s, his young firm already had offices near the wells of Oil City, the refineries of Cleveland, and the shipyards of New York.

crashed and burned, wrecking the luggage but sparing the family. "I... regard the thing as the *Providence of God,*" he wrote home.

People began to wonder if God had provided Rockefeller with special powers. "He sees around the corner," a colleague would say. In truth, Rockefeller posted observers around every relevant corner in his field. Still, Will may have been only half in jest when asking him to stop the rain. Wrote Will, "You can, of course, if you set out to."

In 1867, Henry Morrison Flagler joined the firm, which became Rockefeller, Andrews, and Flagler. "He was a bright and active young fellow full of vim and push," Rockefeller would write in his memoirs, despite being the younger man by nearly 10 years. Flagler, a poor minister's son, had left upstate New York in his youth, as had Rockefeller, and had sold grain to him in rural Ohio. He had also invested in a whiskey distillery with relatives named Harkness. U.S. Senator John Sherman of Ohio, who would confront the oilmen decades later, tipped off the family about a pending tax on distillers. The Harknesses raided a bank's deposits, stockpiled whiskey before the tax, sold it at post-tax prices, and began a march to wealth that would make their heirs leading patrons of medicine, education, and dance. For now, Stephen Harkness, Henry's stepbrother, invested his new riches in the refining firm. Rockefeller shunned liquor but not its profits.

Flagler and Rockefeller worked face-to-face at adjoining desks. They critiqued each other's letters. They walked to and from work together. "It was a friendship founded on business, which Mr. Flagler used to say was a good deal better than a business founded on friendship, and my experience leads me to agree with him," Rockefeller would write.

The firm had many setbacks. Its refineries often caught fire. Its debts reached $250,000 at a single bank. A banker asked Rockefeller to assure the bank's board that the loans were sound. "I answered that I would be very glad of the opportunity to meet the board," Rockefeller later wrote, "as we would require a great deal more money." He got more without the meeting, and bankers began to offer loans unasked. "Wel-l-l," he once replied coyly, "can you give me 24 hours to think it over?" Then he brought himself to take the money.

Soon the partners were the world's biggest refiners. By 1869, they had 900 workers and turned out at least 1,500 barrels a day, or 10 percent of the world's output. Rockefeller tried to keep track of every barrel. "I had a passion for detail which afterward I was forced to strive to modify," he would write. He jotted facts, figures, and ideas in a small notebook: "Don't leave oil in pipes leading from tanks to stills.... Not over 10,000 good barrels on hand and coopers must work *more.*" He also used the notebook to remind people of their promises.

Shipping was slow and expensive then. The oilmen improved it by acquiring their own horses, wagons, boats, and the nation's biggest fleet of railroad tank cars. They also bargained with the nation's growing railroads, which finally spanned the continent in 1869. The railroads were fighting fiercely for customers by offering secret discounts and rebates. Flagler took charge of the talks, but Rockefeller helped in his subtle way. Cornelius Vanderbilt, 74, the haughty steamship king, summoned Rockefeller, 29, to a meeting to discuss shipping oil on Vanderbilt's New York Central Railroad. Instead, Rockefeller sent his business card and waited for Vanderbilt to come to him. Soon Vanderbilt would invest in Standard Oil and rightly predict that his own status as the richest American would someday fall to Rockefeller.

The oilmen also parried with Jay Gould, a ruthless financier who outmaneuvered Vanderbilt for the Erie Railroad and would help Western Union become the dominant telegraph company. Gould, just three years older than Rockefeller, was another mild-mannered New York

Before turning 30, Rockefeller bought a big house on Cleveland's swanky Euclid Avenue. But he chose the street's less fashionable side—home, as the locals liked to say, not to nabobs but mere bobs.

farm boy who shunned liquor and tobacco. His speculations in gold would trigger a nationwide panic and depression in 1869. But perhaps his conquests inspired the oilman's. Rockefeller would tell a friend that Gould was the greatest businessman he had known.

The railroads gave Rockefeller's oil firm rebates of up to 75 percent, plus shares of pipelines linking the wells and the rails. In return, Rockefeller also became a middleman for other refiners' shipments, a first step toward taking over these rivals.

These special arrangements would soon surface and raise outcries that baffled Rockefeller. Buyers bargained in many fields then, as today, and the biggest buyers usually got the best deals. But railroads had special legal privileges, such as the right to seize land for tracks at little or no cost, so they were often said to have special responsibilities, such as charging all customers equal rates. Rebates seemed particularly devious because they created a gap between the posted rates and the effective ones. State laws on the discounts and rebates were varied and unclear. The federal government would not ban such deals for years.

In 1868, the 29-year-old Rockefeller parted with $40,000 of his profits for a recently built home that typified his tastes. It was big and solid but not flashy. It had an iron fence, stone pillars, brick walls, a music room, and five bedrooms, which would soon be more than full. It stood about two miles from downtown Cleveland on Euclid Avenue, a broad, elm-crowned street dubbed Millionaires' Row. He filled his block-deep yard with flowers, trees, and a carriage house. He bought a nearby house that marred his view and gave it to a girls' school a block away. Straining horses spent weeks hauling it there on greased logs. The feat made many spectators and reporters take their first notice of this enterprising young man.

With Rockefeller's help, his church moved to his street and became the Euclid Avenue Baptist Church. He often shook hands with needy worshipers there and slipped them envelopes of money. For decades, even when living out of town, he superintended the Sunday school and Laura superintended its infant classes. The couple also taught briefly at a poorer church. Wherever they served, John's lessons were stern. "Don't be a good fellow," he once said. "Every downfall is traceable directly or indirectly to the victim's good fellowship, his good cheer among his friends, who come as quickly as they go."

Soon all of Rockefeller's siblings had their own families. Their father seldom surfaced, so their mother sold her home and rotated among theirs. The families saw each other often, and John hired Lucy's husband. But John's brother Frank, a rebel by fits and starts, joined John's former commission house, then a rival refinery co-owned by Isaac Hewitt, John's old boss.

The Rockefellers had a second daughter, Alice, in 1869. But she took ill and died 13 months later. Two more girls, Alta and Edith, were born in 1871 and 1872, just 16 months apart. John tried to comfort Laura about this baby boom: "In old age we may be left to lean on the [child] we hoped would delay in coming some time yet." Better yet, that child might be a boy. The Rockefellers were relatively liberated for their era and supported women's schools, including a struggling African-American institution in Atlanta that gratefully became the now-renowned Spelman College. But Rockefeller wanted an heir for his refineries and could not imagine that role falling to a daughter.

This 1876 sign was the first advertising kerosene from Standard Oil.

CHAPTER

3

MISSIONARIES OF LIGHT

In 1870, Rockefeller's firm became the Standard Oil Company, soon to be the world's most famous business name. Standard was an up-and-coming kind of business called a corporation. Corporate investors had special privileges, such as freedom from corporate debts. Critics would argue that investors, like railroaders, had special responsibilities, too.

Rockefeller, now 30, controlled about 29 percent of the private corporation's shares, dwarfing his five partners. He became president; his brother William, vice president; and Henry Flagler, secretary and treasurer. He also served on what was perhaps American business's first executive committee, a small group that made many decisions on behalf of the larger board of directors. At Rockefeller's insistence, Standard's officers drew no salaries at first. They made money only when the business did. "We did our day's work as we met it,... laying our foundations firmly," Rockefeller would write in his memoirs. "None of us ever dreamed of the magnitude of what proved to be the later expansion."

Tycoons such as Jay Gould secretly watered down the value of the stocks they issued. Standard did the opposite, valuing its original shares at a scant $1 million. "Perhaps," Rockefeller would write in his memoirs, "we felt that oil and water would not have mixed." But Standard's dividends, though frugal, would strike critics as exorbitant returns on such low-priced investments.

Meanwhile, the Oil Regions were spewing more crude than the public wanted, and prices were plummeting. Well owners sometimes agreed to quotas but seldom obeyed them for long. Besides, quotas sat shakily with the courts and the public. People had old, sometimes conflicting ideals of fair and free trade. Merchants were supposed to fight cleanly but hard, with few restraints. The ones with the best and cheapest goods would win. The losers would try again or give way to new challengers. Businesses would evolve as scientist Charles Darwin was saying that plants and animals evolved: through survival of the fittest.

But businessmen such as Rockefeller called for a kinder evolution. "I believe in the spirit of combination and cooperation," he would write. "It helps to reduce waste; and waste is a dissipation of power." Cooperative businesses, he argued, would grow bigger and hence more efficient, getting bulk discounts, capitalizing on new technology, improving products, cutting costs, reinvesting profits.

Rockefeller spent months helping to make a secret pool of oil and railroad leaders outside the Oil Regions. They formed a Pennsylvania corporation, half owned by Standard men, and blandly named it the South Improvement Company. South's refiners planned to dictate crude's prices and divvy its shipments among the railroads in return for rebates of up to 50 percent and something even more lucrative called drawbacks—rebates based on rival oilmen's railroad shipping rates. Conveniently, these rates were going to double.

In fact, a clerk doubled them prematurely in February 1872. The Oil Regions' producers rose in fury. Well owners boycotted South's refineries. Mobs blocked shipments, tore up tracks, siphoned off oil, and so deprived Standard that it

Standard Oil's first refinery bordered the Cuyahoga River and Kingsbury Run. It had the essential ingredients for success: water, rails, crude oil, and relentless leaders.

laid off all but 70 of what had fluctuated up to 1,200 workers. Foes called South Improvement Company a "monster," an "octopus," and the "40 Thieves." The chorus spread nationwide. "This corporation has simply laid its hand upon the throat of the oil traffic with a demand to 'stand and deliver,'" cried the *New York Tribune.* South was the "most gigantic and dangerous conspiracy" ever, said the first of many congressional committees to probe Rockefeller's deeds.

The conspiracy fizzled in weeks. Pennsylvania lawmakers revoked South's charter. The pool's railroad leaders hastily met in New York, barring Rockefeller from their room. While he paced outside, they agreed to disband South and promise everyone equal rates. The promise, although quickly broken on the sly, calmed down the Regions for a while.

The public blamed South mostly on Rockefeller and began an obsession with him that would outlast his long life. His pious aggression seemed to be a contradiction; his secrecy, a challenge. Critics would mock him as "St. John" and "John the Baptist." They would denounce him as "The Mephistopheles of Cleveland."

Under attack, his secrecy only grew. He turned reporters away and persuaded his partners to do likewise.

He put a revolver by his bed, posted guards at his home and office, and hired detectives to prevent leaks of business information. He defended himself only to Laura, in passing. "Please say *nothing* only you know your husband will stand by and *stick* to the right," he wrote to her. "A man who succeeds in life must sometimes go against the current.... I feel pleasantly even towards those who have misused me, and will try and not allow all this *noise* and bluster to cause me to yield any vital point." He was also sure of higher support. "It was right between me and my God," he would tell his biographer about South. "If I had to do it tomorrow I would do it again the same way—do it a hundred times."

Rockefeller's silence flustered Flagler. "John," he once cried, "you have a hide like a rhinoceros!" Or perhaps John really had the shell of an oyster. Throughout the South ordeal, he was secretly making a pearl. He was not just pooling rival refiners but absorbing them into what economists call a horizontal monopoly: a company so dominant as to stifle competition in one layer of an industry, such as the refiners who linked oil's producers, shippers, retailers, and other handlers. No one had monopolized as rich a layer as refining before, but perhaps no one had ever matched Rockefeller's daring. He reportedly told another businessman that Standard would eventually refine all the world's oil.

Typically, Rockefeller planned this conquest for a couple of years, then began to execute it with remarkable speed, even compared to today's dizzying pace of mergers and takeovers. From December 1871 through March 1872, he waged what became known as the Cleveland Massacre. He bought out about two dozen Cleveland oil businesses, six of them in two days. He started with the biggest and left almost none behind. He also grabbed two in New York. After a swift purchase, he reportedly gloated, "One more in the fold!" To finance the spree, he took in several new investors, conveniently including bankers and railroad leaders.

ALMOST AN UNFRIENDLY DISPOSITION

On the surface, Rockefeller usually called for gentle business measures. But some colleagues and historians have taken his words as hints for sterner steps. In the following letter to his eventual successor as head of Standard Oil, John D. Archbold, Rockefeller recommended "some kindly way" to coax a railroad that shipped Standard's goods to resume using Standard's Galena lubricating oil. The railroad soon complied.

Aug. 26th 1884

My Dear Mr. Archbold,

I duly received yours of the 21st including a letter from Pres[iden]t. Miller to you of the 19th. I really do not know what we can do in respect to the party you name in your pencil note.

The Lake Shore [Rail] Road are under very great obligations for a large and profitable business and we feel injured that they do not continue using the Galena oil inasmuch as the quality and price favor their doing so. It seems almost an unfriendly disposition although we do not want to cherish such a thought and must persevere in some kindly way to bring them back to their first love.

I beg to return herein the esteemed epistle.

Yours, very truly,

Jno. D. Rockefeller.

Several refiners claimed Rockefeller scared them into selling. "Those who refuse will be crushed," he supposedly said. "You may not be afraid to have your hand cut off, but your body will suffer." But other refiners said he simply, politely explained the truth: The oil business was sinking, and they had to link hands to reach the shore.

Rockefeller saw himself as no less than a savior. "The Standard was an angel of mercy, reaching down from the sky, and saying: 'Get into the ark,'" he would tell his biographer. Never mind that the swelling Standard was helping to raise the waters. And never mind that many rivals shared his love of paddling their own canoes.

Some sellers complained that they got just a fraction of their plants' costs. But others said they got fair prices for their slumping businesses. In fact, like many modern moguls, Rockefeller bought many plants just to scrap them and put them out of his way. Still, Standard's capacity soared to at least 10,000 barrels a day, or one-fourth of the world's output, and its profits soon approached $1 million a year.

Like the great Roman conquerors, Rockefeller turned foes into allies. He offered them Standard stock and often powerful positions. He and Flagler even shared their private office with a former rival. But most of the rivals preferred cash and independence. "They took my money and laughed in their sleeves at my folly," Rockefeller would later tell a reporter. As the stock soared, many of these sellers became his harshest critics, and some broke promises not to compete with him again.

Rockefeller tried to keep abreast of his growing empire. He interviewed all Cleveland job applicants during Standard's early years and seemed to remember all their names. He quietly loomed at their elbows now and then. He told a careful worker, "That's right, eternal vigilance!" He riffled through a clerk's ledger and told him, "A little error here; will you correct it?" The clerk would later say, "I will take my oath that it was the only error in the book!"

Rockefeller promoted good workers quickly and encouraged aides to take the now-popular approach of delegating responsibility. "Get some one whom you can rely on," he told a chemist, "train him in the work, sit down, cock up your heels, and think out some way for the Standard Oil to make some money." He sometimes refused to give advice. "I believe there will be wisdom enough among you gentleman in the lubricating oil business to do the thing that will be best," he once wrote.

Rockefeller was a fatherly boss. He usually paid workers slightly more than the industry average. He offered a partner a year or more of paid sick time. He asked a railroad lawyer to restore permission for an aging Standard employee to tricycle to work along the tracks. He forgave a swindler, kept him on staff, and eventually spent $1,000 on the worker's funeral. He spread shoe-shining kits about the office. He discouraged liquor, tobacco, divorces, and lavish living. His workers seldom struck or even formed unions over the years. But if they tried, the organizers were quickly identified and transferred to new plants.

Rockefeller kept preaching cooperation while conquering. He and Flagler were hooted down at two Oil Regions meetings for proposing pacts between refiners and well owners. He finally arranged a quota in return for price hikes, but both sides broke the deal. "There are some people whom the Lord Almighty cannot save," he would tell his biographer. "They want to go on and serve the devil."

Rockefeller briefly ran two national refining associations in turn, but they became hard to tell apart from his swiftly spreading monopoly. He once learned at noon that he could buy a distant refinery that day for several hundred thousand dollars in cash. He dashed among Cleveland's bankers twice, first asking them to round up the money, then collecting it in time to complete the deal.

An Ohio corporation was not allowed to own properties outside the state. But Standard found other ways to control them. It sometimes leased them or paid them to cooperate. It often bought shares of them for individual Standard partners, who pooled the dividends. These subsidiary companies typically kept their own names, brands, officers, and other vestiges of independence. One subsidiary received a secret drawback for supposedly holding out against Standard. Others bought rivals supposedly to protect them from the monopoly, while really bringing them into its fold.

Some of the subsidiaries' strong-minded leaders kept competing in earnest. One or two were suspected of hiding profits from Standard. At meetings in Cleveland, the growing ranks of partners sometimes swayed Rockefeller on policies or simply outvoted him. But he was usually the first among equals. While they wrangled, he often kept quiet, took notes, or lay on a couch and closed his eyes, then ventured a popular solution.

Rockefeller toured his many companies outside Ohio with the same vigilance he showed in Cleveland. He asked a New Yorker to try sealing a can of oil with 38 drops of solder instead of the usual 40. Thirty-eight proved leaky, but 39 held tight. The reduction of one drop saved hundreds of thousands of dollars over the years, and Standard knew it. It calculated every cost to the fraction of a cent.

The mushrooming corporation opened a four-story headquarters in downtown Cleveland in 1874 and soon expanded it to six. It also persuaded railroads to charge equal rates for all refiners shipping to the East Coast, no matter where the oil was refined, even in distant Cleveland. It was growing big enough to weather floods that swamped rivals. It pioneered self-insurance, saving money to pay for mishaps such as fires. It picked up refineries toppled by an economic slump in 1873. By the decade's end, it refined 90 to 95 percent of the nation's oil. Rockefeller was within a few percentage points of his dream.

Standard was also becoming one of the first vertical monopolies, handling many layers of the same industry. It built pipelines and tank cars to move oil for itself and its rivals. It leased a railroad station in New Jersey for the same purpose. It made more and more refining supplies. It assembled an army of Standard workers who delivered oil in horse-drawn wagons to stores and homes across the country. It assembled a foreign legion that delivered it by oxen, by camels, or on foot around the world. It often supplied instruction pamphlets in the customers' languages.

Standard also developed more than 300 by-products. It made tar and asphalt for America's growing roads, and lubricants for America's rapidly multiplying machines and trains, strengthening its grip on the railroads. It made ingredients for candles, matches, paint, paint remover, and a Cleveland novelty called chewing gum. It took over production of Vaseline and made it a household staple. "We had vision," Rockefeller would tell his biographer. "We saw the vast possibilities of the oil industry, started at the center of it, and brought our knowledge and imagination and business experience to bear in a dozen, in 20, in 30 directions." The only possibilities Rockefeller refused were a kind today's big businesses often try to their regret: ventures into unrelated fields. Standard spent every cent on something to do with oil.

Rockefeller usually tried to keep prices low. While the price of crude fell to about one-fourth of its initial value during his career, he managed to lower the cost of refined to less than one-seventh. "We must ever remember we are refining oil for the poor man and he must have it cheap and good," he wrote to a colleague. Not incidentally, the cuts helped Standard boost sales. It often sold oil at a loss in towns with competition while charging three times more in nearby towns with none. It offered other inducements, too. It sold lamps to homeowners barely at cost and gave discounts to retailers on many items besides oil. Retailers deaf to such inducements met pressures. Standard often shut off their supplies and once opened a cut-rate general store to compete with them.

Standard became notorious for its spies. Sales agents tried to report every independent barrel of oil in their territories. Employees known as "buzzards" followed rivals on sales calls, taking notes and stealing customers. A rival's clerk allegedly sold secrets to Standard.

On the surface, Rockefeller usually called for gentle measures. The champion of cooperation offered to improve or undo several business acquisitions when the sellers complained. He wrote an aide to split a contract between competing bidders: "Give them both a chance to make money." When a railroad's leaders briefly dropped his lubricants, he wrote that Standard "must persevere in some kindly way to bring them back to their first love."

But some employees took his mild words as hints for harsh deeds. "Results were what the master asked for," said one of at least two marketers who quit in disgust with Standard's tactics. "Details he need not know." Besides, Rockefeller often learned about colleagues' ruthless actions without objecting. A partner wrote him about rival refiners, "We will either get them or starve them." And brother Will wrote him, "When we get control of *all* the canning business here it does seem as though the N.Y. refiners would be *in our hands.*"

With sales kits like this one, Standard's many marketers spanned the globe.

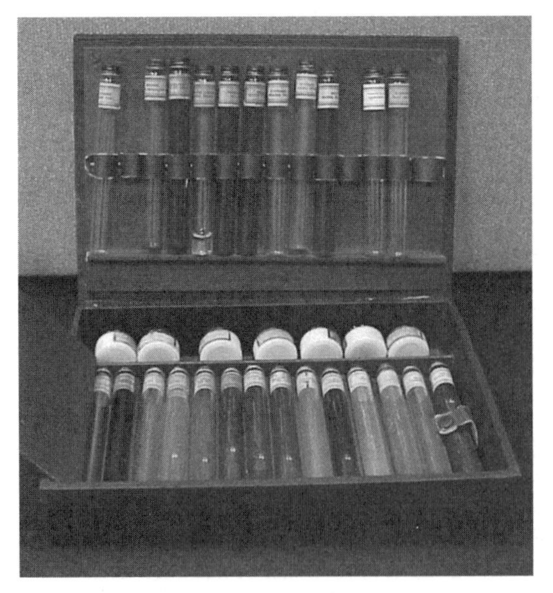

John, too, initiated some harsh deeds. "Pittsburgh refiners should have no chance whatever in any market for local trade oil," he wrote. He especially targeted the many "blackmailing" refiners who seemed to build plants just to sell them to Standard. "A good sweating will be healthy for them," he wrote. He also compromised some of his dearest principles over time. He once told an aide to coax a railroad to break a deal with a rival, despite Big Bill's lessons about the sanctity of contracts. He even made workers toil on Sundays.

Rockefeller was human, after all, and humans usually feel entitled to what they want. He sometimes blamed his victims. "They wanted competition. And when they got it they didn't like it," he would tell his biographer. He often spoke of competition as war, tacitly invoking the old saying that all was fair. He also proved the old saying about the corruption of power, which multiplied his temptations, minimized his punishments, and distanced him from his victims. And he let his lofty ends justify his means. "What a blessing the oil has been to mankind!" he would tell his biographer. He considered Standard's agents no less than "missionaries of light" who drove "the car of salvation."

In fairness, many small refiners used similar pressure tactics, from secret alliances to price wars. But they met with less success and hence less protest. The courts were no clearer on such tactics than on railroad discounts. But Standard's rise made clearer laws inevitable.

Rockefeller achieved perhaps his biggest personal goal in 1874. There were tears in his eyes when he told his partners the news: He finally had a son. Never mind that John D. Rockefeller Jr. had his mother's dark, round features. He was his father's heir all the same. The proud parents, though just 34, had no more babies.

Rockefeller loved to play with his children. He gave them horseback rides. He amused them by catching crackers in his mouth and balancing china on his nose. He once lunged so hard at blindman's buff that he gashed his head and needed stitches. But he was also as strict as his parents had been. Instead of allowances, he gave the children pennies for killing flies, dousing gas lamps, and practicing their instruments. Each child had to donate 20 cents at church every Sunday and pay fines for lateness to morning devotions. Each could eat only one piece of cheese per day. Edith once

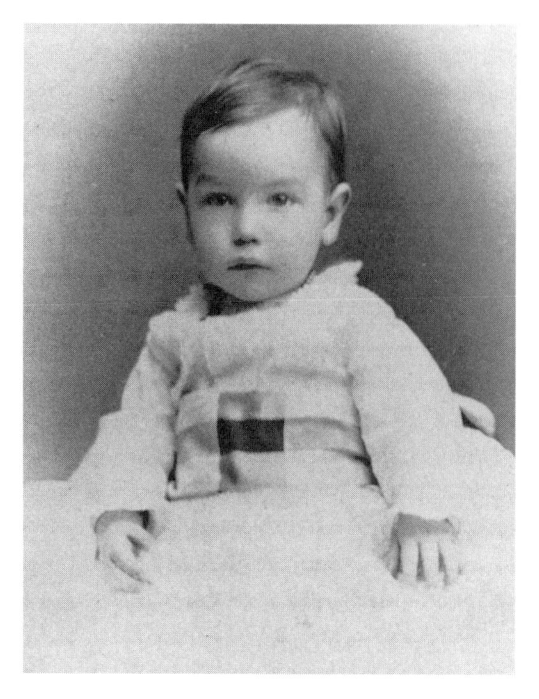

Anxious for a son, Rockefeller promptly entered the name of John D. Rockefeller, Jr., in the new-birth records of Cuyahoga County, Ohio.

snatched the biggest piece. "Edith was selfish," Rockefeller said over and over that day. Still, he matched their savings, foreshadowing his matching grants to charity. He also gave each of them what would amount to several hundred thousand dollars in assets by the century's turn.

By the mid-1870s, Rockefeller was worth more than $1 million on paper and perhaps more than double that in real value. Soon a rare business failure became a family haven. He and other investors built a convalescent home overlooking Lake Erie on the crest of Forest Hill, the first slope of the Appalachians, six miles east of downtown Cleveland. But the financial slump kept the home from opening. So Rockefeller bought it, invited friends to visit his family there, and surprised them afterwards by sending them bills. It seems Rockefeller, despite his love of privacy, somehow meant Forest Hill to be a resort. He soon dropped the idea but spent longer and longer summers in this rambling home, bedecked with turrets and verandas to catch the view. "This quiet country life...carries me back to my boyhood days," he would write to Junior.

Rockefeller furnished the house sparsely, but molded the grounds as lovingly and firmly as his children. He replanted trees up to 90 feet tall to improve his view. He build a half-mile horse track, an icehouse, a limestone quarry, and two artificial lakes, where he let local children skate in the winter. He acquired 16 cows and thousands of chickens. He often returned from work in midday to direct improvements on the grounds, which grew to about 700 acres. "Surveying roads, I have run the lines until darkness made it impossible

Rockefeller, seen swimming in a tree-lined lake at Forest Hill, plunged into his estates as deeply as into his businesses. "In nursery stock, as in other things," he wrote in his memoirs, "the advantage of doing things on a large scale reveals itself."

to see," he would write. Meanwhile, he kept in touch with work on a private telegraph line and soon a telephone line.

His homes were bastions. His family often hosted relatives, friends, and Baptist leaders, but seldom visited them. The children studied with tutors. They did not visit their father's workplaces until adulthood.

The children struggled with headaches and other nervous ailments. Bessie, the eldest, was lively and studious despite poor vision. Alta learned to sing and play the piano well despite losing some hearing to scarlet fever. Edith was willful, and so intense that she cracked Grandma Spelman's rib in a hug. Junior learned to sew and cook with his sisters and wore their mended dresses until he was eight.

Rockefeller's wife had several ailments that worsened over time. In the mid-1870s, the Rockefellers and Spelmans vacationed in Colorado's dry air for her health. But John stayed slim and fit for years. He kept his pulse at a mere 52 beats a minute, about 20 below an average man's. He ate small, slow, plain, lukewarm meals. He snacked on milk, crackers, and barley water. He kept apples on his windowsill. He napped nearly every afternoon, at work or at home. "It is remarkable how much we all could do if we avoid hustling, and go along at an even pace," he would tell his biographer. He took old-fashioned cures, such as eating celery for nerves and smoking herbal pipes for colds. His doctor, Hamilton Biggar, a jovial, dapper Canadian, born the same year as Rockefeller, was perhaps his best friend. Biggar practiced homeopathy: treating sick people with small doses of substances that would make healthy people sick. Rockefeller would continue to subscribe to homeopathy long after his donations to medical research helped to undermine it.

Rockefeller also loved exercise. At work, he tugged at an early exercise machine. He strode barefoot across his lawn. He swam up to a mile at a time, often wearing a straw hat against the sun and leading the children like goslings. He outpaced his neighbors in carriages or sleighs. He guided horses like businesses, calming the jittery ones, making the poky ones sweat, and never sweating himself. He once scraped past a wagon's hubcaps. "That was pret-t-y clo-o-se!" he bragged. But he knew he could not dodge obstacles forever. So he and his brothers bought the family a plot on the crest of Lake View Cemetery, a lush new haven bordering Forest Hill. He spent decades as a cemetery trustee.

Between tending babies, Laura Rockefeller helped to found the national Woman's Christian Temperance Union, which waged war on liquor. Her husband sometimes joined the women in kneeling on tavern floors and praying for the drinkers. He also helped to build an alcohol-free shelter that can be considered Cleveland's first settlement house, a kind of center for social and other services springing up in the nation's cities to help poor and working-class families. Over the years he would spend more than a half-million dollars fighting liquor.

Eliza Rockefeller summered mostly at Forest Hill. "The robins already begin to inquire for you," John wrote his mother one June. He often held her hand during dinner. Big Bill sometimes passed through without warning, bantering with the staff, teaching the delighted children to shoot bows and guns. But Rockefeller's sisters grew scarce. His favorite, Lucy, died at 40, and Mary Ann became reclusive and miserly, even by John's standards. Then again, his brother Frank spent and partied more than enough to make up for her. He also criticized John's refinery takeovers to Congress in 1876. Still, John kept lending him money and hiring his fleet for oil shipments. But Frank was sometimes too busy hunting or drinking to deliver. John finally bought the fleet, and Frank joined a rival refinery. Undeterred, John and Will helped him buy a country estate and a Kansas ranch, then put him on Standard's payroll for more than a quarter of a century. He worked fitfully and quarreled with colleagues.

The Rockefellers' Euclid Avenue home became mostly a stopping point for Sunday dinners and for brief stays in the spring and fall. Rockefeller was spending longer and longer winters working in New York. He began to bring the family along, shipping horses, carriages, and even a piano to and from a Manhattan hotel. The time was fast approaching for this leading businessman to make a permanent home in the nation's business capital.

ORGANIZED UNDER THE MANUFACTURING LAWS OF OHIO

No. 172 — 9 Shares.

STANDARD OIL COMPANY.

CAPITAL STOCK $3,500,000. ALL PAID

35,000 SHARES, $100 EACH.

This is to Certify that W. H. Macy is entitled to Nine Shares of One Hundred Dollars each in the Capital Stock of the Standard Oil Company, transferable on the Books of the Company in person or by Attorney only on the surrender of this Certificate and due payment of all liabilities on the part of the holder to the Company subject to the provisions of Law and the By Laws of the Company. This Certificate is valid only when signed by the President and Secretary.

Cleveland, O. April 29th 1878

Sec'y

Pres't

This 1878 certificate for shares of Standard Oil stock entitled its owner to profits from many subsidiaries, including Socony (Standard Oil Company of New York). Rockefeller wisely told a Standard investor, "Sell everything you've got even to the shirt on your back, but hold on to the stock."

CHAPTER

WHAT SHOULD BE DONE?

By 1877, the Pennsylvania Railroad, which hauled much of Standard's oil, feared the company's rising clout in the transportation field. So a railroad subsidiary began to buy and build big refineries. "Why, it is nothing less than piracy!" Rockefeller reportedly told the railroad's leaders, with no apparent irony. Fighting back, his company, smaller but financially sounder, gave the Pennsylvania the best of sweatings. He denied the railroad oil from the many refineries in his secret grip. He also coaxed friendlier railroads to launch a price war so brutal that the Pennsylvania actually paid to carry some freight.

The warring railroads slashed wages and jobs. Workers replied with one of the first national strikes. Dozens of them died in clashes with militias. Rockefeller did not flinch. He believed wealthy industrialists should cooperate for their mutual benefit, but poor workers should not. "It is hard to understand why men will organize to destroy the very firms or companies that are giving them the chance to live and thrive," he would tell his biographer.

The Pennsylvania finally offered peace for a price. It would sell Standard all its oil properties for $3.4 million. Rockefeller's partners rejected several undesirable ones, so he bought them himself for several hundred thousand dollars. Standard also agreed to become the railroads' peace-keeper, dividing its shipments among them in return for hefty rebates and drawbacks.

Standard now controlled three-fourths of the nation's pipelines and was building more as fast it could. But it could not keep pace with all the new wells. In 1878, it lowered the price it paid for crude and stopped accepting unsold crude for storage at the mouths of its pipelines. The Oil Regions exploded again. Vandals drew skulls and crossbones on Standard buildings. Protestors cloaked in sheets threatened murder. A resident reportedly warned Rockefeller not to visit, or "you will never come back alive."

Other locals retaliated by building long-distance pipe-lines to allied railroads. The Pennsylvania, Standard's friend once again, tore open one of the pipelines. Standard itself countered more subtly. It bought one of the rivals' railroads. It boycotted allied businesses. It leased land in the pipelines' paths. The lines still managed to open, so Rockefeller out-did them. He laid 13,000 miles of pipes to several East Coast cities. His rivals finally agreed to take just 11.5 percent of the pipeline traffic and leave him the rest.

Pennsylvania's state government also fought Rockefeller in court. It indicted him and eight colleagues in 1879 on charges of monopolizing the oil trade. The governor of New York, where Rockefeller was staying at the time, refused to arrest him. The battle was settled with concessions all around, but the war spread to courts and legislatures around the country. A New York legislative committee called Standard's railroad deals "the most shameless perver-sion of the duties of a common carrier" in history. Naturally, Rockefeller thought such probes were out of bounds. "It is not the public's business to change private contracts," he once wrote to Laura.

Standard proved hard to probe over the years. Its leaders burned records, and avoided subpoenas to testify. When dragged before lawmakers or judges, they often spurned questions or gave false answers. Rockefeller issued at least one falsehood, wrongly denying that a particular official of the South Improvement Company had owned stock in Standard. More often, he was just artfully vague and misleading. A prosecutor carelessly asked if Rockefeller had belonged to the "Southern" Improvement Company. Rockefeller denied it and kept his foe off course by adding, "I have heard of such a company." With his magnetic memory, he happened to recall an unrelated company by that name.

"His was the ablest mind I ever encountered on the witness stand," a leading lawyer would say. "He could always read my mind and guess what the next six or seven questions were going to be." Rockefeller testified dully and sweetly, stressing Standard's mission to "light the world." Scoffed *The New York Herald,* "The only thing this company lacks is a chaplain!"

Standard also defused attacks behind the scenes. It helped that the House of Representatives, and later the Senate, included one of Rockefeller's partners and the father of another. Standard made new friends, too. "We want to use all the influence we can command," Rockefeller wrote to a colleague. Standard paid people to testify as supposedly independent citizens. It bought rival lawyers as quickly as refiners. It supported campaigns by Republicans, including, ironically, two who would still become leading foes: Ohio's Senator John Sherman and future President Theodore Roosevelt. It also gave politicians tens of thousands of dollars for personal use, often with Rockefeller's knowledge. Such bribes had not yet been specifically outlawed, but they outraged voters, who expected the officials' undivided loyalties. A mob hung the likeness of a Pennsylvania official carrying a mock check for $20,000 from Rockefeller.

Ironically, Standard started the case that brought its worst publicity. It sued Frank Rockefeller's father-in-law and his partners to enforce an agreed quota for their refinery.

But the courts voided the quota as a restraint of free trade and, worse, let other refiners testify to additional restraints. Nettie Backus said tearfully that Rockefeller, an old friend from church, had seized her late husband's refinery for just 40 percent of its cost. She omitted such details as Rockefeller's having added $10,000 to his appraisers' estimate for the slumping plant and offered later to undo the deal. So did many writers who retold her tale over the years. No other charge "has awakened more hostility against the Standard Oil Company and against me personally," Rockefeller would rightly say in his memoirs.

His press kept growing bigger and harsher. Standard was "the most cruel, impudent, pitiless, and grasping monopoly that ever fastened upon a country," roared the tabloid New York *World*. A new genre called "muckraking" journalism could have been called "oilraking" for one of its favorite targets. Henry Demarest Lloyd is often said to have started the genre by blasting Standard in the prestigious *Atlantic Monthly* in 1881 and later in the book *Wealth Against Commonwealth*. Lloyd made many false charges but truly captured the paradox of free trade: "Liberty produces wealth, and wealth destroys liberty."

Rockefeller claimed that he seldom read his critics. Still, he slowly began to give a few interviews, speaking as dully and sweetly to reporters as to lawyers. "In a business so large as ours... some things are likely to be done which we cannot approve," he told *The World*. "We correct them as soon as they come to our knowledge." Standard also bought some favorable stories, and Rockefeller bought shares of two Cleveland newspapers. But these small steps hardly slowed the attacks.

The bigger Standard grew, the stronger a grip it needed on its subsidiaries. In 1879, Standard formed a new management group. Three employees called "trustees" took over the rights of Standard's 37 investors to vote in the subsidiaries' affairs. But the subsidiaries still proved unruly.

So, in 1882, the corporation secretly created a stronger management group—the Standard Oil Trust—and exchanged shares of it for Standard's old stocks. By written agreement, nine trustees, including Rockefeller, now determined the leaders and policies of 41 companies.

Standard's executive committee, comprised mostly of trustees, voted on every raise over $600 and every expense over $5,000. Specialized committees and employees oversaw production, shipping, and other common work, helping to spawn the 20th century's droves of mid-level managers. These committees and managers would be both a boon and a bane, often stifling initiative. But at Standard they tried to boost it, pooling ideas and giving prizes for success. The trust also slashed duplicate efforts, reducing the number of refineries from 53 to 22 by the mid-1880s.

The law neither recognized nor forbade this kind of trust. The organization was a sort of ghost, manipulating the industry unseen. As its existence slowly came to light, the public widely denounced it and business widely copied it. Trusts arose for many goods, from beef to whiskey. Rockefeller would rightly tell his biographer that trusts "revolutionized the way of doing business all over the world."

Standard Oil's centralized trust needed a centralized headquarters. Rockefeller reluctantly agreed to put it in Manhattan. At 26 Broadway, overlooking New York's harbor, Standard erected a nearly $1 million building 10 stories tall and would gradually extend it to 28 stories. Standard had come of age. It was no longer a sprouting youth in the hinterlands but a mature leader at the nation's hub.

Rockefeller gradually stopped seeing outsiders, which only whetted their curiosity. "We have come to look upon him as a great spider sitting back in his web seeking whom he may devour," a banker said. But he lunched daily with his fellow trustees, characteristically yielding the head seat to a longer-time New Yorker. He also stayed close to his workers and helped them buy stakes in the trust. "I would

Rockefeller saw Standard Oil as a trailblazer, leading the world to prosperity. Critics such as cartoonist Homer Davenport saw the trust and its many followers as savages, trampling rivals and razing democracy.

have every man a capitalist, every man, woman and child," he would tell his biographer.

Rockefeller helped employees from Cleveland find homes in Manhattan and finally became a legal resident there himself. In 1884 he bought a railroad magnate's former love nest: a $600,000 townhouse at 4 West 54th Street. The 20-year-old house was four stories tall, with an early private elevator. It was the opposite of Forest Hill in Cleveland: spare outside and bursting inside with velvet, silk, fashionable paintings, and eclectic motifs from Turkish to Japanese. Rockefeller made few changes. He probably liked the sleigh bed in the master bedroom, and surely liked the safe at its side.

As usual, he improved the yard, this time adding a pond for skating. He often skated in his dress clothes in the morning, then took a nickel ride downtown in an elevated train, jotting notes on the cuff of his shirt, jostling against the poor. He would continue traveling unguarded at times over the years despite growing threats, including a letter bomb intercepted on its way to him and defused. According to his son, Rockefeller said anyone who attacked him in person would suffer for it. He once grabbed a gun and chased a burglar.

The townhouse was on a modest side street, a few yards from swanky Fifth Avenue. The avenue was lined with the mansions of magnates such as William Vanderbilt, railroad heir and Standard stockholder, best remembered for saying, "The public be damned." Three other Standard men had houses at the corners of Fifth Avenue and 54th Street, including Henry Flagler and Will Rockefeller.

John's family joined the Fifth Avenue Baptist Church. Rockefeller became a trustee, and Laura, Alta, and Junior taught there over the years. The family often hosted religious and business associates but otherwise ignored Manhattan society. Rockefeller remained a midwesterner at heart. He used country slang such as "pshaw" and "I declare." He once mocked easterners for viewing Cleveland as "the Wild West where even their lives would be endangered and their talents completely buried."

He sent his daughters to a suburban seminary run by an old teacher of his from Owego. Only Bessie went on to college. She attended Vassar, 80 miles north of Manhattan. It helped that the Rev. Augustus Strong, a Baptist minister from Cleveland, chaired Vassar's board. It also helped that Strong's son, Charles, was courting Bessie.

"Dare to be true," Rockefeller wrote in Junior's autograph book. The short, frail boy struggled to deserve his famous name. He got high grades at four prep schools, including the Browning School, which his father founded with Uncle Will. But he had an apparent nervous breakdown at 13. He rebuilt his strength by helping workers chop logs and break rocks at Forest Hill.

26 Broadway,
New York.

November 28th 1887.

Dear John:

Yours, of the 22nd, duly received. Excuse delay in answering. Have also your telegram of today for the cutter, and will attend to it tomorrow morning. I assume you want the one to carry two persons. I had a pleasant time in Washington. It is a beautiful city. The weather was mild and lovely. After receiving my testi- mony they did not wish any other although they had subpoenaed eight of us. We feel very well

In one of hundreds of letters to Junior over the decades, Rockefeller wrote breezily about a skirmish with federal officials: "After receiving my testimony they did not wish any other."

The father and son were reserved in person but warm in a lifelong series of letters, sometimes more than one a day. "Concur in your decision about painting the storm doors," the father wrote when Junior was 13. "You are monarch of all you survey." He showered the shaky boy with praise. "We are grateful beyond measure for your promise and for the confidence your life inspires." Junior repaid the praise with interest: "If I can be half as generous, half as unselfish, and half as kindly affectionate to my fellow men as you have been, I shall not feel that my life has been in vain."

The Rockefellers' parents lived long lives. But Laura's father finally died in 1881. The Rockefellers hosted his funeral and took in his widow afterward, adding to their home's preponderance of females. Meanwhile, John's mother was slipping and losing her hair, as Rockefeller himself would do later in life. Once, hearing that she was ill, he left a business meeting to comfort her.

By now, Rockefeller seemed to have learned Big Bill's secret. Soon after steering his son to business school, Bill, then 44, had gotten married under an assumed name to Margaret Allen, 20, of Ontario. He eventually moved Margaret to Freeport, Illinois, and began to wander between his wives. For years, Rockefeller tried to separate Bill from Margaret. He gave Bill a ranch in North Dakota and loaned him thousands of dollars over the years, but took steps to keep Margaret from sharing the bounty.

Rockefeller began to travel less for work and more for pleasure. He and his family saw Yellowstone, California, Alaska, and Europe during the 1880s and 1890s. They usually took along physician Biggar and a minister, who led daily Bible sessions. Rockefeller once had so much trouble leaving work behind, he sent for business news from the middle of the Atlantic. But he enjoyed climbing an Alpine glacier and, with the help of interpreters, quizzing the locals. On Sundays, he attended nearby churches and, if impressed, made surprising donations. Still, he spurned beggars and scrutinized his bills, even in French. "*Poulets!*" he once said. "What are *poulets,* John?" Told they were chickens, he checked how many his party had eaten by counting the legs consumed. French or American, the old poultry farmer knew that every chicken had two legs.

At work, Rockefeller sometimes forgot his change purse and borrowed coins from employees. But he insisted on repaying. For a while, he tipped servants by holding out a handful of change and letting them take what they felt they deserved. But he stopped after repeated differences of opinion. He once chided a Cleveland newsboy for lacking change for a dime. The boy became an unusually frugal and wealthy man—comedian Bob Hope.

By the mid-1880s, people were besieging Rockefeller for favors, investments, and donations. "The good people who wanted me to help them with their good work seemed to come in crowds. They brought their trunks and lived with me," he would tell a reporter. "They talked with me at the breakfast table and they rode downtown with me so as to miss no opportunity." They would also deluge him over the years with up to 15,000 letters a week. He weighed their requests with care, trying to do as much good as he could with his more than $100,000 in yearly gifts. "I haven't a farthing to give...to this or any other interest unless I am perfectly satisfied it is the *very best* I can do with the money," he once wrote.

He began to seek cooperation in charity as in business. He gave matching grants: gifts conditional on contributions received from other people. He enriched the Baptists and pioneered what has been called "wholesale charity" by giving a denominational committee hundreds of thousands of dollars to divide among deserving churches and religious schools.

He favored groups that helped people help themselves. "Trying to abolish evils by destroying them at the source, we felt that to aid colleges and universities, whose graduates would spread their culture far and wide, was the surest way to fight ignorance and promote the growth of useful knowledge," the high-school dropout would tell his biographer. He funded colleges from Manhattan to Japan and briefly served on a few of their boards. He particularly helped schools for women, African Americans, and American Indians.

He could afford the largesse. Standard had become the world's biggest and most profitable corporation. In 1885, it had $77 million in net assets and $8 million in yearly profits. It no longer wheedled loans. It financed its own ventures.

Yet Standard was less dominant than before. Its share of refining fell below 90 percent in the early 1880s and stayed below for good, ranging mostly between 75 and 84 percent for the rest of the century. It especially lost ground overseas. Rivals drilled big wells in Russia and Southeast Asia, and two of Europe's leading families, the Nobels and Rothschilds, weakened Standard's grip.

Rockefeller was slow to give up his dream. As late as 1884, he wrote a partner that he still wanted to sell all the world's refined oil. But he seemed gradually to realize that it was too hard to crush every little foe. In what might have been a case of sour grapes, he would deny having held such an ambition. He told his biographer, "We realized that public sentiment would be against us if we actually refined all the oil."

Perhaps needing a new goal, Rockefeller dropped his long resistance to owning many wells. Pennsylvania's output of crude oil had leveled off in the early 1880s, reportedly leading a Standard man to suggest that the company find another industry. Rockefeller pointed upward and replied, "The Lord will provide." Sure enough, in 1885, big wells began to gush near the northwestern Ohio town of Lima (pronounced *lye*-ma). Lima's sulfurous oil smudged lamps, rusted machines, and offended noses. But, if the Lord provided it, Rockefeller would use it. He proposed spending millions for drilling rights in the Lima region. A partner leaped to his feet and shouted, "No!" Rockefeller calmly pledged up to $3 million of his own money. The partner backed down, saying, "I guess I can take the risk if you can."

Soon Standard chemists patented a way to remove the sulfur with reusable copper oxide. Before long, the trust was drilling from Pennsylvania to Indiana, pumping a third of America's crude oil, completing its vertical monopoly, and frightening foes more than ever. It was also boosting the now-huge field of industrial science. It tested shipments in laboratories at several points along the way. It worked to lower what were several thousand deaths per year from kerosene fires and explosions. It helped to develop safer lamps and stoves and teach customers how to use them properly.

Science helped and hurt Standard by turns. The lightbulb, invented in 1879, began to displace kerosene lamps. But natural gas, a by-product of oil wells, especially in Lima, grew popular for stoves, streetlights, and furnaces. Standard built interstate gas lines and won many municipal franchises, sometimes through bribes or tricks. Officials in Toledo, Ohio, split a franchise between two supposed rivals that both turned out to belong to Standard.

Soon the new internal combustion engine was powering machines and vehicles across the country with the help of lubricating oil and the once-unwanted gasoline. Standard would serve Henry Ford's first car and the Wright brothers' first successful plane. It would also open the world's first public gas pump.

Attacks on big business kept rising meanwhile. Crusaders of various stripes, from populists and progressives to socialists and anarchists, demanded fairer opportunities for average Americans to share in business's soaring wealth. The major political parties vowed to stop the trusts' abuses.

An Ohio lawsuit reversed an 1885 drawback and revealed that a Standard clerk had urged a railroad to "please turn another screw" against a rival. *The New York Times* said the case proved Standard's "meanness... greed, injustice, and oppression." Meanwhile, rivals in Buffalo, New York, accused Standard men of trying to blow up their lubricants plant. Two defendants were convicted on minor charges despite revelations of wrongdoing by their accusers. In a rare outburst, Rockefeller rose and cried, "What should be done with people who bring an action against men in this way? What should be done?" Then he shook his fist and strode from the courtroom.

In 1887, Congress finally required equal rates for all railroad freight customers. For enforcement, it created the Interstate Commerce Commission, the first of many federal regulatory agencies. But by then Standard depended more on pipeline and tank car receipts than railroad deals. The company would be convicted of illegal rebates 20 years later, but acquitted on appeal.

In 1890, under rising public pressure, Congress passed the Sherman Antitrust Act, which banned "trusts and combinations in restraint of trade and production." Senator Sherman's bill had so many holes that it was nicknamed the "Swiss Cheese Act." At first it was used more to curb unions than businesses. Still, it was Congress's strongest statement yet that it could regulate private business for the public good.

The same year, Republican David Watson, Ohio's attorney general, sued Standard of Ohio for being a puppet of the New York trust. Mark Hanna, Rockefeller's old classmate, now a powerful Republican, reportedly sent Watson an unsubtle warning: "Regarding you as in the line of political promotion, I must say that... litigation of this character is a great mistake." But Watson persevered.

In 1892, the Ohio Supreme Court ordered the local Standard to leave the trust. Instead, the trust dissolved, but only on paper. Its investors took shares in Standard's various companies, elected their directors, and kept running them as parts of a whole. Standard Oil of New Jersey, conveniently located at 26 Broadway in New York City but chartered under liberal New Jersey laws, gradually became what was called a holding company, owning control of the other Standard firms. The trust had lasted just 10 years, but "trust" became a lasting synonym for monopoly.

Meanwhile, rivals kept fighting Standard in the field. In 1892, Pennsylvanians formed what gradually became the Pure Oil Company, with wells, pipelines, refineries, and European distributors. Railroaders linked to Standard attacked a Pure Oil construction site with burning coals, boiling water, and a cannon. Standard itself fought with price wars and a takeover bid. Yet Pure Oil somehow survived, making a small but telling dent in Standard's grip.

Rockefeller faced ups and downs at home, too. A lamp he claimed was filled not with Standard's oil but alcohol exploded in his townhouse in November 1888, burning Laura's face and hands. Bessie, 22, finally married Charles Strong at the townhouse the following March. She gave up Vassar and the church for Strong, an agnostic who took her to Germany so he could study philosophy there. A few days before the wedding, Eliza, 76, took sick at Will's. Big Bill sent word that he was too sick himself to visit her. She died later that month. Rockefeller hosted her funeral on Euclid Avenue and asked the minister to call her a widow. But he had her buried in the family plot with room at her side for Big Bill. He still hoped his father would end his wanderings there some day.

Rockefeller's own health faltered for a couple of years. Now in his early 50s, he had bronchial, digestive, and nervous ailments, perhaps including ulcers. "A little more of that would have killed him," Dr. Biggar would recall. Rockefeller had also contracted alopecia, a rare glandular disease still little understood that causes hair loss throughout the body.

He recuperated by twice avoiding the office for months at a stretch. He also toiled with farm crews at Forest Hill

The two John D. Rockefellers learned to ride bicycles, which had become a nationwide craze in the 1890s. Junior struggled for years to keep up with his famous father in sports, business, and charity.

and plunged into the popular new exercise of bicycling. He mastered such stunts as jumping on a moving bicycle. Although an expert called the project impossible, Rockefeller consulted engineering books and laid out a navigable bike path to Forest Hill's summit. He gave visitors bicycles and strenuous lessons. He left them behind, panting and lost, on mad spins through the woods.

Benefactor Rockefeller makes a rare visit to the University of Chicago. Beside him is his approved choice for university president, William Rainey Harper.

CHAPTER

I Can't Endure to See That Money Idle

Rockefeller blamed his ailments on charity. "I investigated as I could, and worked myself almost to a nervous breakdown in groping my way, without sufficient guide or chart, through this ever-widening field of philanthropic endeavor," he would write in his memoirs. Reverend Strong, Bessie Rockefeller's father-in-law, wanted $20 million from the tycoon to create a Baptist university in Manhattan. But a young, passionate minister, Frederick T. Gates, conducted a survey showing greater need for a Baptist school in booming Chicago.

Rockefeller liked Gates's scientific approach and was still a midwesterner at heart. In 1889 he pledged to give $600,000 (nearly $10.9 million today) to help establish the University of Chicago if other donors gave $400,000. He helped to choose the trustees and the president, the brilliant Rev. William Harper, who had earned a doctorate from Yale at 18. The university opened in 1892, with Rockefeller's son-in-law Charles Strong on the faculty. Two Rockefeller aides soon joined the board of directors. Small wonder that *Life* magazine called the school "Ye Rich Rockefeller University." When university president Harper fired an economist who had criticized a Standard company, critics said Rockefeller was destroying academic freedom.

But Rockefeller really seems not to have influenced the firing or many other academic decisions. The University of Chicago fast became famous for independent, acclaimed scholarship. It took students of all faiths, genders, and colors from the start and soon cut its ties to the Baptist Church. It hired top professors from other institutions faster than Standard bought refiners. Rockefeller chafed at the mounting debts but kept supporting the school. In 1895, football coach Amos Alonzo Stagg, running the nation's first collegiate department of physical education, announced a $3 million gift from Rockefeller at halftime of one game. His players rallied from a 12-10 deficit to a 22-12 win, boosting Stagg toward a national record for victories that would last for decades.

Rockefeller first visited the university on its fifth anniversary. Students regaled him with a ditty: "John D. Rockefeller, wonderful man is he / Gives all his spare change to the U. of C." Said Rockefeller, "The good Lord gave me the money, and how could I withhold it from Chicago?" He would give the school some $35 million over the years, and donations from his son and the family's charities would more than double the figure.

In 1891, Rockefeller plucked Reverend Gates from the pulpit to guide his donations. Tensions often arose between the trim, terse Rockefeller and the longhaired, expressive Gates, but they shared passions for divinity and dollars. Gates found that Rockefeller was funding many bumblers or swindlers. He began to require written applications, to interview the most promising applicants, and to recommend only what seemed to be the very best causes to Rockefeller.

In 1892, Jay Gould died, and Rockefeller inherited his reputation as the world's richest and most hated man. The oil tycoon was worth some $100 million by then, but his

The University of Chicago quickly outgrew its original plans and budget. Rockefeller, its frugal founder, covered the school's losses for a while but gradually weaned it from his support.

investments were surprisingly careless, often in uninspected properties recommended by friends. He began to have Gates check these holdings as well. Many proved to be worthless or fraudulent. Gates sold what he could, took over a dozen or so other businesses, and made one quite profitable.

Relieved, Rockefeller gradually stopped working on Saturdays and prepared to retire. Many of his closest Standard colleagues had already left or died. Flagler was busy building resorts in Florida's eastern swamps and inspiring gossips. He bribed state legislators to pass a law that let him divorce his insane second wife, then married a third less than half his age. A mortified Rockefeller seems to have stopped socializing with him.

But the depression of 1893 kept Rockefeller at work. He loaned its victims nearly $6 million and, rather than sell depressed investments, borrowed millions in turn from

Standard. The company also loaned the government $10 million and weathered the slump with ease.

By lowering prices, the slump helped Rockefeller expand a good investment: newly discovered iron mines in Minnesota's Mesabi range. Like Ohio's crude oil, the Mesabi's powdery ore seemed useless at first, exploding when used to make steel. Then the steel plants adjusted to the ore, and its price soared. A backwoodsman charged that Rockefeller had bilked him in a Mesabi purchase, but he retracted the charges for a payment of $525,000. Soon Rockefeller had the world's biggest ore fleet to transport the raw material to steelmaking plants: 56 ships plying the Great Lakes.

Steel king Andrew Carnegie grew leery of this new competitor. The jealous Carnegie, once a clerk for Rockefeller's

Cartoonists often portrayed oil king Rockefeller and steel king Andrew Carnegie as fierce competitors in wealth and benevolence. Rockefeller eventually won on both counts.

leading foe at the Pennsylvania Railroad, privately called the oilman "Rockafellow" and "Wreckafellow." Newspapers often ran box scores comparing the nation's two leading tycoons and benefactors. The pair regularly exchanged Christmas presents: for the steel king, a paper vest worth pennies; for the teetotaler, a bottle of fine whiskey. But Rockefeller sent wholehearted congratulations to Carnegie in 1896 upon the opening of what would become one of about 2,800 Carnegie libraries around the world: "I would that more men of wealth were doing as you are doing with your money," wrote Rockefeller, "but, be assured, your example will bear fruits."

The same year, Carnegie offered to do business with Rockefeller's mines, railroads, and vessels if Rockefeller promised not to make steel. The cooperative Rockefeller agreed. "Don't you know," Carnegie would tell the Senate years later, "it does my heart good to think I got ahead of John D. Rockefeller on a bargain." In fact, the treaty helped both men. Rockefeller's ore stocks soared 16-fold in the seven years he owned them.

The 1893 depression also helped Rockefeller piece together a rural retreat in New York to outdo Ohio's Forest Hill. The new retreat bordered his brother Will's estate and took the name of Pocantico Hills from its rustic village, which lay about 23 miles north of Manhattan in Sleepy Hollow country, the domain of fiction's Headless Horseman. Expanding Pocantico with his usual zeal, Rockefeller bought and razed a village nearby, and he surrounded a home with huge shade trees to make its owner sell. John Junior later relocated a railroad and a college for further expansion. Eventually, the estate encompassed nearly five square miles.

As usual, Rockefeller paid more heed to exteriors than interiors. He took a modest old house with a view of the wide Hudson River. He built a swimming pool, a huge carriage house, and gorgeous gardens. He let the public walk, bicycle, or ride horses through much of the estate but not squander gasoline there.

Rockefeller began to shuttle between Manhattan and Pocantico during the cool months. In the warm ones, he kept visiting Forest Hill and eastern resorts. He often took friends and relations along and left Laura behind, because trips seemed to strain her health as much as they refreshed his. She was becoming frailer and fussier. When home, Rockefeller spent much time at her bedside: bringing her flowers, reading to her, coaxing her to let her window be opened wider.

Other relatives were struggling as well. Laura's mother died in 1897, at age 87. Rockefeller's father, Big Bill, was losing his sight, hearing, and waistline, although he still popped up at times like a ghost, embarrassing his son with crude jokes. Brother Frank began to pop up, too, threatening John and demanding forgiveness for loans. After a few refusals, Frank stopped speaking to him for the rest of their lives. But he had only begun to tell the press, wildly and vaguely, about "my brother's long record of heartless villainy." With typical ambivalence, he loudly uprooted his children's coffins from the family plot and quietly reburied them just 200 yards away. Still, the brothers' families remained close, and John secretly helped Will save Frank from bankruptcy twice.

Will embarrassed John, too. He and a Standard partner used their dividend checks to manipulate other companies' stocks. The press blamed the schemes of the so-called Standard Gang on the company. Still, John continued to visit Will and travel with him often.

As for John's children, Bessie's ailments worsened in chilly Chicago, so she and her husband Charles moved to New York, where Rockefeller endowed a chair in philosophy for him at Columbia University. Edith married a Chicagoan, Harold McCormick of McCormick reaper wealth, and soon took a mansion there with him. The couple wrestled for years with depression and debts, thanks to such luxuries as Edith's $2 million string of pearls. On the good side, Edith and Bessie both made Rockefeller a grandfather in 1897, the year he turned 58.

Daughter Alta helped to form several charities in Manhattan and Cleveland, including a community center near Forest Hill that became Alta House. But she had trouble finding a man to her father's liking. At about 20, she fell in love with her 47-year-old pastor. Rockefeller persuaded him to leave Cleveland.

John Junior became class president at Brown University and managed Brown's football team out of a deficit. The ever-competitive John Senior once raced along the sidelines at a Brown game, cheering. Shedding his old objections, he even hosted a dance at Brown.

In 1896 the economy was rebounding from its recent slump, and a cautious Republican, William McKinley of Ohio, defeated a populist Democrat, the fiery William Jennings Bryan, for President. McKinley's campaign was managed by Mark Hanna and bankrolled by big businessmen, including Rockefeller, who gave $2,500, and Standard's board, which gave a hefty $250,000. The reassured Rockefeller dropped his last real duties at Standard by mid-1897. But he still owned nearly 30 percent of Standard stock, and colleagues insisted that he officially head the dominant Standard Oil of New Jersey. Never mind that he attended no meetings and drew no pay. "If any of us had to go to jail," an envious partner told a reporter, "he would have to go with us."

The empire's real leader became John D. Archbold. Nine years younger than Rockefeller, he had gone from being a staunch rival to a staunch ally. Short, slim, as volatile as oil, Archbold reminded people of Napoleon, whom Rockefeller once said would have made a great businessman. Archbold often brought an apple and business news to Pocantico. But he showed his independence by boosting dividends, sharply cutting operations at Cleveland's refineries, and cutting Frank Rockefeller's pay. He gave friends lavish bribes and foes lavish insults, such as "stinking liar" and "miserable whelp." He seldom agreed to compromise with investigators. His imperious ways helped to hasten the monopoly's demise.

Rockefeller got gentler help from Junior, who finished Brown and joined Standard's headquarters in 1897, at $6,000 a year. The retired father never said what the son should do. Junior filled inkwells for a time, but soon began to help Gates with Rockefeller's charities and investments. He also lost almost a million dollars borrowed from Rockefeller to a Wall Street trickster. His father questioned him at length and promised to cover the loss. Junior fared better in arranging a fitting family monument at Lake View Cemetery for $16,000: a huge, spare obelisk of gleaming white granite, 66 feet tall and weighing 357,000 pounds.

In 1899 Rockefeller found a new obsession: golf. He was pitching horseshoes or rope rings called quoits in his typically calm, smooth way at a resort in Lakewood, New Jersey, and a friend said the oilman would be good at the growing game of golf. Trying out the newly popular sport, Rockefeller hit his first three golf shots straight but barely 100 yards long. "Do not some players send the ball farther?" he asked. He was hooked.

He began to learn the game from professionals. He studied his swing in photographs and a new medium called moving pictures. Unlike ordinary players, who tend to shift and jiggle as they line up shots, he stood motionlessly over the ball until ready to swing. Aides staked his foot with a croquet wicket and shouted, "Keep your head down!" as he swung. In case these precautions failed to keep his shots straight, the frugal sportsman used old balls near water hazards.

He built a 12-hole course at Pocantico and a 9-hole one at Forest Hill. He golfed daily in almost any weather. He wore a pith helmet on hot days and a paper vest on cool ones. Aides held an umbrella over his head and shoveled

Rockefeller's obelisk at Lake View Cemetery is characteristically big and simple.

snow from the course as necessary. To save his energy, they handed him a bicycle after each shot and, as he aged, began to push it for him. The game made him more sociable. He played with acquaintances and bantered between shots.

Rockefeller turned 60 in the last year of the 19th century. The 20th began unevenly. His first grandson, John Rockefeller McCormick, died at Pocantico from scarlet fever in 1901, before turning four. One of the four other McCormick children would die young, too. But Rockefeller's family grew in 1901, when Alta, 29, married lawyer E. Parmalee Prentice, and John Junior, 27, married the lively Abby Aldrich, whose father, Nelson, was a powerful, conservative Republican senator from Rhode Island. Both couples honeymooned at Pocantico and took townhouses across from Rockefeller's in Manhattan. Bessie's only child was a girl, but Junior and Alta followed Edith's example in naming their first boys for grandfather John Senior.

Rockefeller grew closer to Junior's spouse than to Alta's. He sent legal work to Parmalee at first, but cut back when the fees seemed too high. Still, he gave all his children allowances that started at $30,000 a year. They also asked him to support pet charities and pay for luxuries, such as Chinese porcelains. He sometimes refused or stalled for a while, but usually came through in the end.

In 1901 the new U.S. Steel Co. became the nation's first billion-dollar business, surpassing Standard in assets. The upstart's leader was one of Rockefeller's closest rivals in wealth, Wall Street baron J. Pierpont Morgan. Rockefeller, at his brother Will's estate, had once met the highborn, red-nosed Morgan, who would bequeath scholars a lavish Manhattan library. The result had been mutual dislike. "I could see that Mr. Morgan was... very haughty, very inclined to look down on other men," Rockefeller would tell his biographer.

In forging U.S. Steel, Morgan bought Andrew Carnegie's steel mills and sought Rockefeller's iron empire. Humbling himself, he asked to visit Rockefeller's office. The retired oilman invited him to his townhouse instead. When the guest mentioned iron, his host referred him to John Junior's office. Junior helped to negotiate the deal so coyly that Rockefeller reportedly said, "Great Caesar, but John is a trump!" Soon Junior would represent his father on charitable and corporate boards, including Standard's, and Rockefeller would tell golf partner, "My greatest fortune in life has been my son."

A middleman also helped work out the iron deal: Henry Clay Frick, a Carnegie colleague, wounded by a radical, remembered today partly for his Fifth Avenue

On the golf course, Rockefeller poses between his physician, Dr. Hamilton Biggar, a native Canadian, and the mayor of Compiègne, France.

mansion, which has become a museum housing his leading art collection. There was a natural rapport between Frick and Rockefeller, both humbly born and soft-spoken, but harsh about business when they thought it necessary. Rockefeller had once sent Frick congratulations for having detectives shoot strikers. Now, to elude the press, the two men met after dark behind shrubs at Pocantico. Soon they closed the deal for $88.5 million, mostly in U.S. Steel stock. Rockefeller Senior and Junior served on the company's board for a while but eventually sold their shares, partly to protest what they considered to be extravagant dividends.

Shortly before the iron deal, Rockefeller suddenly lost his remaining hair, even his eyebrows. He bought wigs of different lengths and wore them in rotation, as if his hair were growing. He facetiously credited the new hair to crude oil treatments, boosting sales. But the wigs looked fake and often slid off-center. Editorial cartoonists mocked his new looks, which were grimmer than ever. He mocked himself, too, boasting of a new car, "I can do 50 miles an hour in that machine without turning a hair!"

Meanwhile, he began to have osteopaths manipulate his spine. "Listen to that, doctor," he reportedly said when his vertebrae cracked. "They say I control all the oil in the country and I haven't enough even to oil my own joints." But his health was strong enough overall for another ambition: If he could not gain a 100 percent monopoly in business, perhaps he could live for 100 years. He even vowed to golf with Dr. Biggar at that age.

To help keep the vow, Rockefeller sought a flatter, warmer golf course than the ones at his estates. In 1902 he bought a country club with a three-story clubhouse called Golf House on 75 wooded acres in Lakewood, New Jersey, about 9 miles west of the Atlantic and 49 miles south of Manhattan. He began to spend a few weeks there every spring and fall en route between Pocantico and a winter resort in the golfing mecca of Augusta, Georgia. He expanded the new estate and bought a nearby cottage for Bessie and her family. She was faltering in body and mind, becoming as miserly as her Aunt Mary Ann and worrying about dying poor, of all things.

Rockefeller's three estates were big businesses, producing much of what they consumed, including food, electricity, and gas. They reimbursed each other for goods exchanged. "We make a small fortune out of ourselves," he would write in his memoirs. He employed hundreds of seasonal workers at each home, monitored them with care, and guided the early careers of promising ones, such as Cyrus Eaton, future industrialist and peace champion. A supervisor once fired a young rider for letting a horse stumble. Rockefeller rehired the boy, arranged riding lessons, and said, "You have to make a horse know you are boss."

Retirement paid well. Rockefeller made $58 million from investments in 1902. He only wished he could find charities that used his wealth wisely. He once borrowed back a gift at 6 percent that the University of Chicago had put in an account without interest. "I can't endure to see that money idle," he wrote to Gates. Humorist Finley Peter Dunne mocked this compassion for cash, calling Rockefeller a "society f'r th' previntion of croolty to money."

Some reformers thought the government should redistribute wealth. But Rockefeller doubted that the people's representatives would fund them wisely. "It is the duty of men of means to maintain the title to their property and to administer their funds until some man, or body of men, shall rise up capable of administering for the general good the capital of the country better than they can," he would write in his memoirs. By then, he had begun to create such bodies himself—independent charities of stunning scope.

Rockefeller resented the government's taxes, regulations, and investigations. But critical publications such as The Verdict *magazine portrayed him as holding the government in the palm of his hand.*

CHAPTER

Shall We Go On, Gentlemen?

Rockefeller's first independent charity was the Rockefeller Institute for Medical Research in New York City, now Rockefeller University. He planned it for several years, but opened it in 1901, soon after his first grandson's fatal illness. He gradually gave it $61 million. It was the nation's first organization purely for medical research. It grew cautiously and stayed within its budgets, unlike the University of Chicago. It drew criticisms for animal experiments but plaudits for many breakthroughs. It discovered blood-typing and isolated antibiotics. It proved that DNA transmits hereditary traits and that viruses can cause cancer. It trained or employed doctors who won 19 Nobel Prizes.

The Reverend Gates and Rockefeller Junior sat on the boards of the institute and of future Rockefeller charities as well. Rockefeller gave the pair nearly free rein and visited the institute just once. Still, he read about its cures with care. Wrote Gates, "I have seen the tears of joy course down his cheeks as he contemplated the past achievement and future possibilities."

Rockefeller next began to form "benevolent trusts," as he would call them in his memoirs. "If a combination to do business is effective in saving waste and in getting better results, why is not combination far more important in philanthropic work?" His were not the earliest such trusts but they were among the most influential, bringing research and efficiency to many new fields.

He started with the General Education Board. He consulted several experts about it, including pioneering African-American educator Booker T. Washington, who had won a scholarship decades earlier from Rockefeller's Cleveland church. Congress chartered the board in 1903 with an unusually modern mission: to promote American education "without distinction of race, sex or creed." Gradually getting nearly $130 million from Rockefeller, the board backed thousands of new high schools, demonstration farms, medical schools, and other programs, mostly through matching grants. It had its critics, though. Southern whites resented the mostly northern group for helping the region's African Americans and hiring some of them to carry out its work. Liberals resented the board for funding segregated schools, especially ones that steered African Americans toward manual labor. And politicians tried harder and harder to squeeze the source of its funds.

In 1900, President McKinley handily defeated Bryan again. The next year, a deranged radical from Cleveland assassinated McKinley. Rumors followed of a violent plot against tycoons. Instead, there were legal attacks. The new President, Theodore Roosevelt, liked to say, "Speak softly and carry a big stick." But he attacked monopolies both with fiery speeches and big sticks. He filed dozens of suits under the Sherman Antitrust Act, with more success than ever. He also coaxed Congress to authorize penalties for unequal shipping rates, whether from railroads or pipelines. An angry Senator Mark Hanna started to challenge him for the Republican nomination in 1904 but died that February. Standard's leaders reluctantly supported Roosevelt, who won a full term and hit them harder than ever.

Yet Roosevelt considered himself a moderate who wanted just to curb big business's abuses, not its legitimate work. He coined the term "muckrakers" for business's even harsher foes in the press. Two magazine serials that became books during his terms in office scorched Standard. "Frenzied Finance," which began in *Everybody's Magazine,* blasted the Standard Gang's stock schemes. Author Thomas W. Lawson acknowledged Rockefeller's distaste for the schemes but blamed them on Standard and "the Rockefellers" anyway. In passing, he called Rockefeller a machine "diagrammed in the asbestos blueprints which paper the walls of hell."

By popular demand, the leading *McClure's Magazine* stretched "The History of the Standard Oil Company" from 3 to 19 installments. Author Ida M. Tarbell, *McClure's* managing editor, was the daughter and sister of Standard foes in the Oil Regions. She was a childhood neighbor of a renegade Standard partner who slipped her information. She was also a biographer of Rockefeller's hero, Napoleon. She wrote about Standard's conquests more calmly and convincingly than most muckrakers did. She acknowledged Rockefeller's "marvellous genius" and Standard's "consummate ability." But she retold, with little rebuttal, the widow Backus's claims of having been underpaid by Rockefeller for her late husband's refinery. She documented the company's espionage, price wars, and courtroom evasions, writing that "Mr. Rockefeller has employed force and fraud." And she urged the public to rein in business, "for it is *our* business."

Rockefeller called his latest foe "Miss Tarbarrel" in private, but refused to discuss her in public. "Not a word about that misguided woman!" he told a friend. His health held up fairly well under her blows, but most of his family faltered. Laura had an apparent stroke and would spend the rest of her life mostly in beds or chairs. Bessie, Edith, and Junior fled to Europe with various ailments.

The press had begun to tar Junior as well as his father. It accused him of both boosting his father's plunder and lacking his genius. "Without virtues as without vices, he is the sublimation of the mediocre," wrote *Cosomopolitan* magazine. Rockefeller fumed to a friend, "I don't mind what they say about me and other rich men, but I resent their attacks on my son!"

In 1905, soon after her father died, Tarbell attacked his old foe in a two-part profile that dropped all pretense of fairness. She blasted Rockefeller's look of "concentration, craftiness, cruelty, and something indefinably repulsive." She blasted Forest Hill as "a monument of cheap ugliness." She also started a media dragnet by saying his father, Big Bill, had disappeared.

The truth was Big Bill was bedridden in Illinois, where Rockefeller seems to have secretly visited him. He died soon afterward, at age 95, and was buried there. The New York *World* exposed his bigamy in 1908. Undaunted, his second family raised a monument with his fictitious surname. In 1917, Rockefeller finally gave up hope of burying Bill next to his first wife, Eliza, and moved her beside his own reserved space.

The press also played up Rockefeller's 1905 gift of $100,000 to a missionary board of Laura's old denomination, the Congregationalists. Many ministers and politicians denounced this "tainted money." U.S. Senator Robert M. La Follette of Wisconsin called Rockefeller "the greatest criminal of the age." But for once the potshots seemed to fall flat. "Sure John D's money is tainted," vaudeville comedians replied. "'Tain't for you and 'tain't for me!" Mark Twain wrote to *Harper's Weekly* in the character of Satan, claiming credit for the wealth behind most charity: "Since the Board daily accepts contributions from me, why should it decline them from Mr. Rockefeller, who is as good as I am?" In a more wholehearted show of support, 400 businessmen visited Forest Hill to praise their host.

Fighting tears, he pointed to a flag above the house and said they had picked a perfect day to come: the 50th annual Job Day, commemorating his first full-time work.

Although the government's attacks kept growing, Rockefeller's reputation slowly seemed to rise. Standard helped by renouncing its silence and issuing articles and books in praise of itself. Rockefeller helped by golfing, bicycling, and traveling with reporters. He conceded that business needed bounds: "Capital and labor are both wild forces which require intelligent legislation to hold them in restriction." He clucked about having been "made into a sort of frightful ogre, to slay which has become a favorite resource of men seeking public favor." But he looked forward to better days: "You newspaper men can do much toward making some of us better acquainted with the others."

Rockefeller was positively mellowing. He began to dress more showily, sometimes in a yellow silk coat. He caught glimpses of the sinful theater. He even built a small amphitheater at Forest Hill for amateur plays.

He developed a steady but restful routine in retirement. He generally rose at 6 a.m., read a newspaper, then rambled through the house and gardens, giving workers nickels and dimes. At 8, the family and guests gathered for a blessing, meditation, Bible passage, and breakfast. After the meal, he lingered at the table for his digestion and passed the time playing Numerica, a competitive sort of solitaire. As a good Baptist, he used numbered tiles, not cards. He gave nickels to the losers and dimes to the winner—often himself, in which case he transferred a dime from his right pocket to his left. He also gave dimes to guests for well-told tales and servants for extra chores, such as cleaning up spills.

At 9:15, he tried, as he told one guest, "to keep the wolf away from the door." That meant reviewing his letters, investments, and gifts. Typically defying public opinion, he devised a formula for selling stocks on the rise and buying them on the wane. He borrowed up to $20 million at a time for investments, including shares in the fledgling General Motors Corporation. He also erected an early Cleveland skyscraper called the Rockefeller Building. A shady financier later renamed the building for himself. An irked Rockefeller had Junior buy it back and undo the change. The move proved good for the building when the financier went to prison. In another deal, Rockefeller spent $40 million vainly trying to help Jay Gould's son, George, gain a railroad empire. But George led him to a better investment in banking that would help Rockefeller's heirs control Chase Manhattan Bank.

At 10:15 a.m., Rockefeller played nine holes of golf. At 12:15 p.m., he bathed, then napped. At 1, he ate lunch and played more Numerica. At 2:30, he lay on a sofa and heard letters read aloud. Then he took a ride in an open automobile, wearing goggles against the wind. He often urged his

An older Rockefeller enjoyed daily rides in a series of cars, including this Ford. As a widower, he also enjoyed the company of women.

chauffeur to pass cars and set records for the trips. In mellower moods, he stopped to lounge on the grass, query bystanders, pluck wildflowers, or pick up hitchhikers.

After the ride he took another nap. At 7 p.m. came dinner and yet more Numerica. At 9 p.m., he listened to live music, chatted with guests, or dozed in a chair. At 10:30, he retired, usually with a book of sermons. He would hardly change the schedule over the years, except to gradually lengthen the rests and shorten the golf.

Rockefeller heaped his multiplying grandchildren with kisses, coins, and advice, especially against waste: "Be careful, boys, and then you'll always be able to help unfortunate people." Several of them grew to have well-publicized troubles in school and romance. Senior sometimes chided them, but kept giving them money, even over their parents' objections. "We are responsible for his failings, and God have mercy on us all," he wrote to Alta about her wayward son.

The Rockefellers visited Bessie's sickbed in France in June 1906. Her death came in November at age 40, the same as her Aunt Lucy. Four days later, the federal government sued Standard for alleged rebates, espionage, and other restraints of trade. Soon 6 more federal and 21 state suits followed. Ohio alone filed 939 indictments. Rockefeller often tried to dodge subpoenas in these cases. He hid his whereabouts. He avoided his telephone in case it was tapped. His aides searched delivery trucks and swept the lawn with spotlights to reveal anyone trying to sneak in to serve legal papers.

Competitors posed new challenges meanwhile. Bigger wells than ever were sprouting from Illinois to California, spewing more crude oil than even Standard could control. By 1911 the monopoly's grip shrank to 14 percent of the nation's crude oil and 70 percent of its refined product. Overseas, Standard had long sought alliances with either of its leading rivals, Royal Dutch or Shell, but the two teamed up in 1907 and eventually surpassed Standard.

In July 1907 Rockefeller lost coat buttons in the crush of people outside a courtroom in sweltering Chicago. Inside, he was grilled in vain by Judge Kenesaw Mountain Landis, a future commissioner of Major League Baseball, who was as tall and imposing as his name. Rockefeller said he hardly knew how Standard's new leaders made a living. Crossing his legs, adjusting his cane, he finally conceded, "They have a refinery, and refine oil."

The jury found Standard guilty of illegal rebates on 1,462 carloads of oil, each conceivably punishable with a $20,000 fine. Then Landis repaid Rockefeller for his absurd testimony. On the day of sentencing, Rockefeller calmly began his usual golf at Forest Hill, with a reporter from Cleveland's *Plain Dealer* in tow. Soon a messenger darted up with the news. Rockefeller gave the boy a dime, read the message, pocketed it, and said, "Well, shall we go on, gentlemen?" Then he hit his ball 160 yards down the middle of the fairway.

"How much is it?" a partner finally asked.

"$29,240,000, the maximum penalty, I believe," replied Rockefeller. He pointed to the tee. "It is your honor. Will you gentlemen drive?" Despite the record fine and later rainfall, Rockefeller shot his best round to date, 53 for nine holes, although he would outdo it a few years later by 14 strokes.

Before the round was over, Rockefeller added, "Judge Landis will be dead a long time before this fine is paid." Sure enough, Standard was acquitted in a retrial. But the government kept pressing its other cases. Roosevelt invited Rockefeller to the White House to discuss them. Pleading ill health, the retiree deferred to Standard's real boss, Archbold. But he was healthy enough to fight a stock market crash variously blamed on him, Roosevelt, Landis, or the Standard Gang. Rockefeller used millions to bail out Will, Edith, the market, and the government, fueling his reputation's rise.

Puck *magazine shows Standard Oil as a slithery octopus with the government in its grip. But the law would eventually sever those tentacles.*

The next boost was a rambling memoir that debuted in *The World's Work* magazine in 1908. It ran for seven installments, then became a book, *Random Reminiscences of Men and Events.* Publisher Frank N. Doubleday interviewed Rockefeller and did most of the writing, with critiques by the tycoon's staff. "I am tempted to become a garrulous old man, and tell some stories," the memoir said in Rockefeller's name. He praised his parents, partners, and charities. He waded into some controversies and skirted others. He denounced "needless competition" for "introducing heartache and misery into the world." And he forgave his foes unasked: "I have had at least my full share of adverse criticism, but I can truly say that it has not embittered me, nor left me with any harsh feeling against a living soul."

His reviews varied. The *Indianapolis News* paraphrased him as saying, "Once upon a time a Christian young man... put [rivals] out of business for the good of the public." He got better reviews for telling a publishers' luncheon about his medical institute in 1908. "Mr. Rockefeller got up and talked sweetly, sanely, simply, humanly, and with astonishing effectiveness, being interrupted by bursts of applause at the end of almost every sentence," wrote Mark Twain, a publisher on the side.

The same year, Rockefeller testified across the street from Standard's headquarters at 26 Broadway in one of the federal suits. "John D. Rockefeller's memory was bright as a coin from the mint while his own lawyer was interrogating him," wrote the Wheeling *Register.* "But on the third day, when the government counsel began a cross-examination, he hadn't a memory as long as a shoestring." Still, steadier witnesses showed, once and for all, that Standard kept many supposedly independent companies from competing. The address of one such company turned out to be the back door of Standard's headquarters.

Nineteen hundred and eight was also the year tabloid king William Randolph Hearst revealed many of Archbold's bribes. Although Junior had known about some of them before, he asked Rockefeller to fire Archbold. Rockefeller refused. So Junior asked to resign as Standard's vice president. Rockefeller agreed. From then on, the son fulfilled his heritage more in charity than business.

High-Class Dealing

After decades of reserve, an elderly John D. Rockefeller grew chatty. His memoirs ran in The World's Work *magazine from 1908 to 1909. In 1909 they were published as a book entitled* Random Reminiscences of Men and Events. *The following is a typically wholesome excerpt.*

The underlying, essential element of success in business affairs is to follow the established laws of high-class dealing. Keep to broad and sure lines, and study them to be certain that they are correct ones. Watch the natural operations of trade, and keep within them. Don't even think of temporary or sharp advantages. Don't waste your effort on a thing which ends in a petty triumph unless you are satisfied with a life of petty success. Be sure that before you go into an enterprise you see your way clear to stay through to a successful end. Look ahead. It is surprising how many bright business men go into important undertakings with little or no study of the controlling conditions they risk their all upon.

Forgive me for moralizing in this old-fashioned way. It is hardly necessary to caution a young man who reads so sober a book as this not to lose his head over a little success, or to grow impatient or discouraged by a little failure.

Rockefeller was still playing golf in 1931, the year he turned 92. He liked to chalk his driver so he could see where it struck the ball.

CHAPTER

Our Splendid, Happy Family Must Scatter

In 1908, Rockefeller supported William Howard Taft, another temperate Ohio Republican like McKinley, to defeat the tireless Bryan and succeed Theodore Roosevelt as President. Taft won, and escalated the war on monopolies. The next year, a circuit court ordered Standard Oil of New Jersey to split into competing companies. Appeals staved off the end until May 15, 1911. Then the bulky Edward D. White, chief justice of the United States, spent 49 minutes mumbling through a bulky opinion of 20,000 words. He finally said Standard had taken "undue" steps "to drive others from the field and exclude them from their right to trade." Seven justices agreed. The eighth wanted all such steps banned, undue or not.

Standard had six months to break up. Word reached Rockefeller on the links again, this time at Pocantico. He told his golf partner, a local priest, to buy Standard stock. He never read the fatal opinion but sent colleagues a mock obituary: "Dearly beloved, we must obey the Supreme Court. Our splendid, happy family must scatter."

Standard became 34 separate companies, with its investors taking proportional shares of each. Standard of New Jersey finally let Rockefeller retire. He proved right about the empire's stocks. The public, allowed to buy them for the first time, seemed to crave Standard's tainted money. For several years, the companies benefited from both lingering mutual cooperation and growing competition. Despite Rockefeller's love of size, Standard's bloated bureaucracy had often stifled initiative before the breakup. Now an unshackled scientist at Standard of Indiana invented a new way of "cracking" crude under pressure to boost its yield of gasoline. The companies' net worth rose fivefold in the next 10 years, and Rockefeller's tripled in the next two, peaking in 1913 at an estimated $900 million (about $14.9 billion today). He was now the world's richest man by far.

"Your fortune is rolling up, rolling up like an avalanche!" Gates had already written him a few years earlier. "You must distribute it faster than it grows! If you do not, it will crush you and your children and your children's children." It helped in 1909 when the tycoon launched the $1 million Rockefeller Sanitary Commission, which tamed hookworm, a scourge of warm climates. It helped even more when he proposed the wide-ranging Rockefeller Foundation. For a couple of years, Congress balked at chartering it, afraid that it would scatter money that prosecutors were seeking in fines. But New York finally chartered the foundation in 1913 "to promote the well-being of mankind throughout the world."

The new foundation gradually got a $183 million endowment and gave the earnings to many innovative programs, from world peace campaigns to an early movie library at an institution spearheaded by Abby Rockefeller, New York's Museum of Modern Art. Like other Rockefeller charities, the foundation mostly focused on health. It spurred the growing fields of psychiatry and molecular biology. It funded medical schools from Brussels to Peking. It fought malaria, typhus, tuberculosis, and many other diseases. It lost six researchers to yellow fever but developed a vaccine for the contagion.

The New York World *admired Rockefeller's sure footing, if little else about him. By the time of this 1908 cartoon, Rockefeller's face was so famous that* The World *saw no need to identify him.*

Nineteen thirteen was also the culmination of another long-planned work. For all his love of engineering, Rockefeller had never commissioned his own home. But he had lost his Pocantico house to fire in 1902. So he took another one on the grounds and asked Junior, who had his own lodge at Pocantico, to build him a new house at the summit: a 500-foot knoll called Kykuit (*kyke*-it, from a Dutch word for lookout). An architect submitted lavish plans. Rockefeller ignored them. Junior perceptively had them scaled back. Rockefeller approved them with a few more revisions. He rejected a showy central staircase, for instance, and repositioned the house so each room would catch sunlight at desirable times, such as during meals but not naps. To do so, he spent days at the site, sitting with a big model of the house on a turntable that he rotated with levers.

Kykuit House was completed in 1908. The eclectic home had a rustic exterior of fieldstone and a citified interior of intricate plasterwork. It had an elevator, a pipe organ, and gorgeous views. But it turned out to have been scaled back too much, even for Rockefeller's tastes. It echoed with noise from the elevator, plumbing, and delivery entrance. So workers overhauled it from 1911 to 1913. They expanded the third floor. They added a fourth. They faced the front with rich carvings. Rockefeller designed his favorite change himself: putting the delivery entrance in the basement, beneath a tunnel of stones.

Soon, to the dismay of Rockefeller and other tycoons, the federal government levied its first income tax, using a sliding scale of up to 6 percent. By then Rockefeller was also giving more and more money to his children, especially Junior, who once got three checks of $500,000 in a week. "What a delightful habit you are forming!" the son replied. Rockefeller even gave him the Euclid Avenue house. According to a lawyer on hand, Laura said, "Why, John, we are deeding our little nest!" John patted her hand and replied, "That's all right. We still have a few nests left!" By 1922, he had left himself a mere $25 million or so, while his daughters had trust funds of $12 million and his son owned an unrestricted $500 million.

He saw Junior not as his beneficiary but his fellow benefactor. Rockefeller wrote a memo for his heirs saying he wanted "to have my fortune used, as he has used it and as I know that he will continue to use it, for the benefit of mankind." Junior promised to comply. "I can only hope and pray that I shall be as conscientious in my stewardship as you have always been in yours, and I shall strive to be as wise and generous," he wrote. He also strove to reciprocate Rockefeller's gifts, with mixed results. He offered a Rolls Royce, but Rockefeller took the cash value instead and gave it to charity. He also tried a fur coat. "I did not feel that I could afford such luxuries," Rockefeller replied, "and am grateful for a son who is able to buy them for me." He soon returned the coat to Junior, who wore it for years.

Edith asked to help run the family charities. Rockefeller ignored her. He may have thought it took manly arms to move heavy sums. He may also have balked because of her continuing personal troubles. She spent years in Switzerland getting treatment from famed psychiatrist Carl Jung. At her urging, Rockefeller read up on psychiatry and philosophy but gained no enlightenment. "I keep to a simple philosophy and almost primitive ideas of living," he wrote. She also urged him to open up: "There is warmth and love in your heart when we can get through all the outside barriers which you have thrown up to protect yourself." Replied Rockefeller, "I can think of nothing which I would more devoutly desire than that we should be constantly drawn closer." But she resented his occasional pointers. "How sadly they need your presence," he wrote about her children. "I am not lecturing. I am not scolding. I love you, Edith dear; and I am still hoping."

By then, a relatively small investment had caused one of the family's worst debacles. Rockefeller had spent $6 million for control of Colorado Fuel and Iron. Junior was a director, and Gates's uncle, L. M. Bowers, was chairman. The United Mine Workers struck the company in 1913. Hundreds of workers were dying each year in accidents, and the rest were repaying most of their wages to live in company towns.

With Junior's support, the company spurned the union and evicted the strikers. An armored car killed several of them in October. The next spring, Junior told Congress that he would rather see workers die than have a compulsory union. A proud Senior gave him Colorado stock. A week later, guards shot more workers and razed their tents with burning oil. Hidden beneath the canvas, two women and eleven children suffocated.

Soon radicals were threatening Junior's life. Some died from a bomb reportedly meant for him. Others smashed windows and razed a barn at Pocantico. Senior strode toward them one day, hoping to calm them down, but guards coaxed him back.

Junior decided to seek fresh advice. He hired an early master of public relations, Ivy Lee, who would create the trademark Betty Crocker character and the Wheaties "Breakfast of Champions" slogan. Junior also had the Rockefeller Foundation, which he headed, commission a peace plan from W. L. Mackenzie King, a future prime minister of Canada. King proposed joint committees of workers and managers to resolve grievances. Junior toured the mines to win the workers' support for the committees and made a balking Bowers resign. Gates resentfully scaled back his work for the family. But Junior stood his ground. "I believe it to be just as proper and advantageous for labor to associate itself into organized groups... as for capital to combine for the same object," he told a federal panel. Impressed by his calm testimony, Senior gave him yet more stock. The federal government criticized the foundation for helping a family business and eventually banned company-sponsored unions as shams. But they were still a step forward for the Rockefellers.

Rockefeller spent the winter of the Colorado crisis at Forest Hill with Laura and Lute, who were too sick for the usual trip to Pocantico. At the Euclid Avenue church, he said, "The best thing I ever accomplished and the thing that has given me the greatest happiness was to win Cettie Spelman." The family finally left town in February 1914, after Ohio's tax-listing day, when the state government considered everyone in residence to be fair game for property taxes. Soon came a last government prosecution of Rockefeller. Ohio tax commissioners demanded $1.5 million for property also taxed in New York. He avoided a subpoena by summering at Pocantico with Laura, Lute, and the unwelcome Colorado protestors. The Rockefellers celebrated their 50th anniversary and 75th birthdays there. Then Laura seemed to improve, so Rockefeller and Junior vacationed in Florida during the winter. On March 12, 1915, they got two telegrams close together. The first said Laura was dying. The second said she was dead. "Mrs. Rockefeller just slept on," an attending nurse wrote in a journal, "with a look of the most perfect peace and comfort and happiness lighting her face as she passed into her Heavenly Home."

For the first time, Junior saw Rockefeller cry. Then an accident forced the already shaken men to switch northbound trains. At Pocantico, Rockefeller stared at Laura's body for a long time. "Her face bore that angelic radiance," he wrote to Edith. After a funeral there, he stored Laura's body at a local cemetery for months. Finally, a new Ohio governor fired the tax commissioners and quashed their claim. Now Rockefeller could return to the state without legal danger. Carefully eluding the press, he brought Laura home to Cleveland and buried her at Lake View at sunset. "All was quiet and peaceful as Mother would have had it," he wrote to Junior.

Soon Rockefeller honored her memory with a $74 million foundation called the Laura Spelman Rockefeller Memorial. The fund supported churches, missions, and early research in the social sciences for several years, then merged with the Rockefeller Foundation. In all, he would give a record sum of about $530 million to charities, including some $447 million to those he founded.

Meanwhile, World War I boosted the popularity of the foundation and its founder. Together, they spent $70 million supporting the allied cause. Rockefeller also let volunteers grow vegetables at his estates and roll bandages in the Manhattan home, which he seldom used any more. Crowds cheered his once-hated name at war bond rallies. The king of Belgium thanked him at Kykuit for food for his starving kingdom. For once, governments encouraged the oil industry to cooperate in fueling military vehicles. Rockefeller relished the irony: "There must have been a Providence ruling over these aggregations of great funds which have been used with such conspicuous benefit in helping to liberate the world," he told his biographer.

The biographer was William O. Inglis, a *New York World* editor hired by public relations adviser Ivy Lee. Starting in 1917, Inglis interviewed Rockefeller an hour a day for more than two years. The writer transcribed 480,000 words that were surprisingly playful, angry, modest, and boastful by turns. Rockefeller called Standard's rise "one of the most remarkable, if not indeed the most remarkable, in the annals of commercial undertakings." He rued his old reserve: "Our silence encouraged the wildest romancers to spread wild tales about us." Inglis also interviewed many of Rockefeller's relatives and associates. But experts such as Ida Tarbell said the resulting biography was more flattering than convincing. Junior consigned the text and transcripts to the family archives, but researchers still use them as the best account of at least Rockefeller's side of his story.

The longer Rockefeller lived, the more friends and family he lost. After some 20 years of being denied Frank's company, John saw him buried in 1917. In 1922 he took the last of several trips to his old haunts in upstate New York with Will, who died a few days later of throat cancer and pneumonia despite the Rockefeller Institute's help. Lute died in 1920, and Mary Ann, Rockefeller's last sibling, in 1925. He even outlived the younger Archbold and Gates. He also survived Dr. Biggar, who died 13 years before his date to golf with Rockefeller at 100. "We must close up the ranks and press forward," Rockefeller wrote to Junior after another such loss.

Rockefeller also lost a home. A fire of unknown cause razed the house at Forest Hill in 1917. He seems never to have visited Ohio again, even to bury relatives or visit their graves. He was still bitter about the tax suit. "Cleveland ought to be ashamed to look herself in the face when she thinks of how she treated us," he told Inglis.

Rockefeller replaced his losses as best he could. After the death in 1913 of his scandalous old partner Flagler, Rockefeller felt safe in wintering at a Flagler hotel in Ormond Beach, Florida, just north of Daytona Beach. In 1918 he bought a home across the street called The Casements. The three-story, gray-shingled house was plain, of course, but gave the sort of view he loved: of flowered terraces spilling to the Halifax River. He also found a hostess to replace Laura and Lute: the hearty, jocular Fanny Evans, 30 years his junior, a relative from Cleveland's outskirts.

He reached a lifelong goal in 1920, when the 18th Amendment banned alcohol. But bootleg liquor and mob wars resulted. So he did not object when Junior supported the ban's repeal in 1933. Meanwhile, he helped to consolidate members of the many Protestant sects into what were ironically called union churches. He attended the Ormond Union Church and helped to found the Union Church of Pocantico Hills, later famous for stained glass windows by two leading artists, Marc Chagall and Henri Matisse. Junior helped in turn to build perhaps the leading such establishment, Manhattan's Riverside Church, and to found the National and World Councils of Churches.

Edith, like her Uncle Frank, did not see Rockefeller for roughly the last 20 years of her life. Midway through that period, on the verge of divorce, she returned from Europe and asked to bring her reputed lover to Golf House. Rockefeller agreed only to see her alone. She consented, stood him up, promised to come another time, but never did. She died of cancer in 1932, six days before her 60th birthday.

Despite his losses, Rockefeller seemed to grow more cheerful and open with age. He roamed Ormond Beach alone. He asked to be called "Neighbor John." He threw parties, crawled among the children, and tooted party horns with them. He joked with adults. A friend bragged that his car got 18 miles to the gallon. "You will ruin me!" the oilman replied. A golfer fell backwards during a swing. Rockefeller recommended "a feather-bed attachment."

At Ivy Lee's suggestion, Rockefeller began to give an estimated 20,000 to 30,000 coins to strangers. He coupled the coins with advice and blessings, such as "God Bless Standard Oil." Recipients often treated the coins as lucky charms, displaying them on walls or in jewelry. His handouts were also featured in newsreels at the nation's multiplying movie theaters. The new star liked to show off for the cameras. He once posed in a taxiing airplane for his supposed first flight, although his fearful valet would not let the plane take off.

In 1923, Rockefeller tips a caddy barely bigger than the golfer's clubs. "We should not rejoice in the downfall of others, but I slaughtered four men at golf on Saturday last," he once wrote in a letter. "This was very wrong, and of course I will never do it again."

Sometimes Rockefeller seemed to be having the adolescence he had missed the first time around. He flirted with women in his car and sometimes pinched or poked them. "That old rooster!" a woman cried after fleeing. "He ought to be handcuffed." But most people back then considered "old roosters," especially rich ones, more funny than shameful.

At other times, Rockefeller seemed neither young nor old but ageless, as if he had already reached the heaven of his faith. "Here is a man at peace with God," said famed painter John Singer Sargent, who depicted him twice. In a voice growing high and thin, he often crooned hymns such as "Jesus Wants Me for a Sunbeam." "He wasn't singing *to* anyone, especially," his grandson, David Rockefeller, the retired president of Chase Manhattan Bank, has written in his memoirs. "It was more as if just a feeling of peace and contentment were welling out of him." Rockefeller even gave out copies of an original poem:

> I was early taught to work as well as play;
> My life has been one long, happy holiday
> Full of work, and full of play
> I dropped the worry on the way
> And God was good to me every day.

Rockefeller kept playing the stock market, sometimes with money borrowed back from Junior. In 1929, the worst depression yet whittled his fortune to a mere $7 million. He still tried to rally the nation again. He gave money to the unemployed, bought a million shares of Standard of New Jersey, and signed a statement written by Lee: "Prosperity has always returned, and will again." It returned fastest to Rockefeller. In 1935, he got $5 million from his life insurance policy for reaching the then rare age of 96.

He seldom ventured from the warmth of Lakewood or Ormond Beach any more. But he watched from a distance as Junior spread the family's name and wealth around. The son helped to revive the economy by building Manhattan's Rockefeller Center, still billed as the world's biggest privately owned complex for business and entertainment. He supported scientific progress, as his father did, but also preservation. Instead of uprooting trees, he gave thousands of acres of them to the National Park Service. He built the Cloisters medieval museum in Manhattan and restored colonial Williamsburg in Virginia. He also reluctantly backed Abby's Museum of Modern Art and razed the family's townhouses to make room for it.

The Great Depression revived resentment of the rich, but Rockefeller's press kept improving on balance. In the 1932 book *God's Gold,* John T. Flynn wrote that Rockefeller's was "the least tainted of the great fortunes of his day." In 1937's *John D. Rockefeller,* B. F. Winkelman wrote that "his methods of accomplishment bear up rather better than most." Junior had long sought another authorized biographer but balked at the roughly $250,000 advance demanded by Winston Churchill, Britain's future prime minister. Allan Nevins of Columbia University finally took the job free, although Junior paid for help with research. The result was *John D. Rockefeller: The Heroic Age of American Enterprise,* published in 1940. Toward the end of his 1,430 pages, Nevins summed up his protagonist: "By virtue of his organizing genius, his tenacity of purpose, his keenness of mind, and his firmness of character, he looms up as one of the most impressive figures of the century which his lifetime spanned."

In 1933, Rockefeller strolls among the sheep at his estate in Lakewood, New Jersey. He was always a watchful shepherd, whether of animals or people.

Rockefeller never read those words. In his 90s, his weight fell below 90 pounds. His rides, strolls, and rounds of golf dwindled. He kept nurses, oxygen tanks, and other medical aids at the ready. He saved his strength for one last goal. "I've tried to do what good I could and I really would like to live to be a hundred," he told Ormond Beach's mayor. He kept entertaining guests and directing home improvements meanwhile. On May 22, nearing his 98th birthday, he paid off the mortgage of his Cleveland church's new home across Euclid Avenue. Then came a fitful night. "Raise me up a little bit higher," he told a nurse. "That's better." Soon his hardened heart stopped beating. He died at 4:05 a.m. on May 23, which was one of his beloved Sundays. He had missed his goal of 100 years even more narrowly than a 100 percent monopoly. But he died confident of reaching an even dearer goal. He had told automotive genius Henry Ford a few years earlier, "I'll see you in heaven."

Death brought Rockefeller his highest praise yet. "A great man with a great vision," said James A. Farley, a leading politician. "World Citizen Number One," said Samuel Untermyer, a leading courtroom foe. A private train car took Rockefeller's body to Pocantico. During his funeral, the old Standard companies around the world conspired again—this time restraining trade for five minutes of silence. Then, for the first time in 20 years, he returned to Cleveland. His coffin was laid beneath an underground concrete dome at Lake View, with Laura and Eliza forever at his sides. Nearby were many old friends and foes, such as Mark Hanna, Maurice Clark, the widow Backus, the Spelmans, and Dr. Biggar. Biggar and Rockefeller would golf no more but would be together at 100 after all.

Rockefeller Center, built in the 1930s, dwarfed midtown Manhattan at first. A controversy promptly arose when workers destroyed a left-leaning mural including Vladimir Lenin by famed Mexican artist Diego Rivera.

Rockefeller's estate was worth $26 million. The bulk of it went for the taxes he loathed. The rest went mostly to Bessie's only child, Margaret Strong, whose mother had died too soon to pass along a fair share of his money. In all, he left behind 2 children, 13 grandchildren, and 11 great-grandchildren. His son kept the "Junior" in his name until dying in 1960, at 86. "There was only one John D. Rockefeller," he often explained.

What survives Rockefeller today? As of 2000, The Casements and Kykuit were still intact, and three of his Manhattan rooms survived as installations at museums. His Cleveland headquarters had vanished, and a bigger building with new occupants had swallowed those in New York. But several structures still bore his name, including Cleveland's Rockefeller Building and Manhattan's Rockefeller Center, which remained partly in his family.

British Petroleum had swallowed a few of Standard's old companies, including its flagship in Ohio. But several Standard survivors remained independent and prominent, including Pennzoil and Chevron. And Standard's two biggest branches, later known as Mobil and Exxon, merged again in 1999, forming the world's biggest publicly traded oil company, although with just a fraction of Standard's old market share.

Other industries were consolidating at record rates, often disproving Rockefeller's faith in the efficiency of size. The government has tolerated most of these monoliths, but was fighting a headline-making war against Microsoft, the computer software giant, which had come to rival Standard's market share.

Junior roughly matched Rockefeller's records for wealth and charity, and other magnates have shattered them. Of his personal charities, the General Education Board has long been inactive, but the Rockefeller Foundation, Rockefeller University, and the University of Chicago still rank high in their fields.

His descendants continue to lead the nation not only in his favorite fields of business and philanthropy but also in art collection, which the patriarch ignored, and government, which he resented. Nelson Aldrich Rockefeller, inspired to greatness partly by sharing his paternal grandfather's birthday, became New York's governor and the nation's Vice President. Nelson's brother, Winthrop, became governor of Arkansas. Nelson's nephew, John D. (Jay) Rockefeller IV, became governor of West Virginia and later a U.S. senator.

What a Providence!

Few correspondents have been as faithful for as long as John D. Rockefeller and his son, John Jr. The father's letters were usually briefer and milder than the son's but still convey plenty of praise, as below:

September 12, 1918

Dear Son:

Answering yours of the 9th, you could not have enjoyed the visits of the past two weeks which we have had together more than I did.

You are very busy, but you never seem too busy to put yourself out to come and visit me. These visits I appreciate more and more, and I don't tell you so nearly as much as I ought to.

What a Providence that your life should have been spared to take up the responsibilities as I lay them down! I could not have anticipated in the earlier years that they would have been so great, nor could I have dreamed that you would have come so promptly and satisfactorily to meet them, and to go beyond, in the contemplation of our right attitude to the world in the discharge of these obligations.

I appreciate, I am grateful, beyond all I can tell you. There is much for you to accomplish in the future. Do not allow yourself to be overburdened with details. Others must look to these. We will plan and work together. I want to stay a long time to help do my part. I hope you will take good care of your health. This is a religious duty, and you can accomplish so much more for the world if you keep well and strong.

Affectionately,
Father

Rockefeller poses with Junior's family about 1916. Rockefeller had four daughters, then a son. Junior had a daughter, then five sons.

What of Rockefeller's verdict in history? Writer after writer continues to ponder it. Rockefeller "cheated and lied his way to a great fortune" but was still "the most upright of all American industrialists," wrote David Freeman Hawke in 1980 in *John D.* "So much good had unexpectedly flowered from so much evil that God might even have greeted him on the other side," wrote Ron Chernow in 1998 in the acclaimed *Titan*.

Rockefeller's legacy also lives on at his plot in Lake View. Thanks partly to funds from his descendants, the staff keeps the grass green, the ivy trim, and the obelisk gleaming. Visitors often reciprocate Rockefeller's gifts and seek his blessings by leaving coins on his monument and headstone.

Rockefeller Family Tree

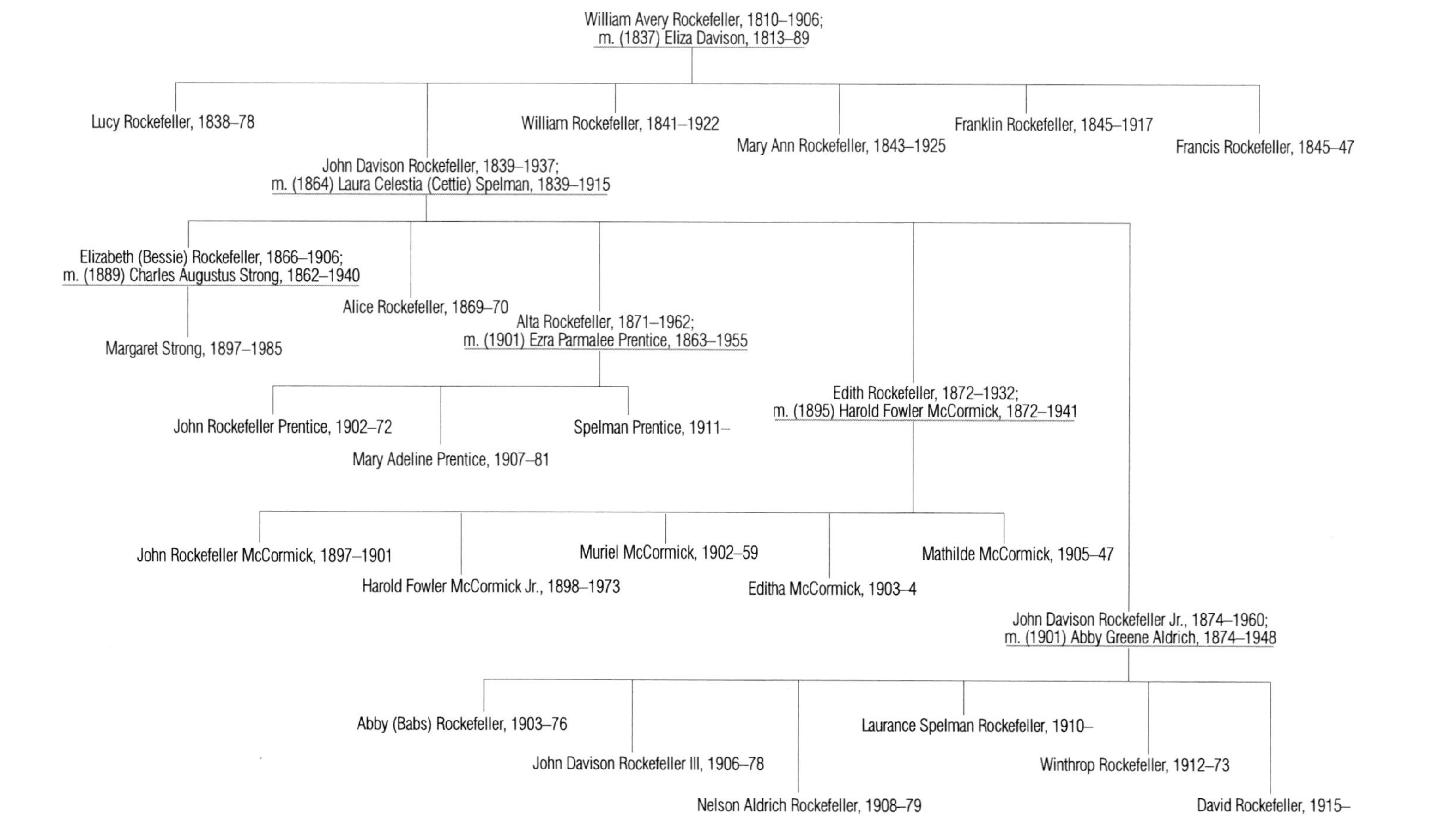

CHRONOLOGY

1839
John Davison Rockefeller is born to William Avery and Eliza Davison Rockefeller in Richford, New York

1855
Leaves Central High School in Cleveland; attends business college; starts work in wholesaling

1859
Helps to open Clark and Rockefeller commission house

1863
Helps to start Andrews, Clark, and Co., an oil-refining firm

1864
Marries Laura Celestia (Cettie) Spelman

1865
Buys out most of his refining partners; brings his brother William into the firm

1866
His first child, Bessie, is born

1867
Takes Henry Morrison Flagler into the firm

1870
Helps to incorporate Standard Oil Company

1872
Efforts to pool the oil industry are shouted down, but he quietly buys out many rivals

1874
Gets a long-sought male heir: John D. Rockefeller Jr., the last of four surviving children

1877
Occupies Forest Hill, a country estate outside Cleveland; sparks a deadly railroad strike

1879
Is indicted for stifling competition, with decades of prosecutions to follow

1881
Henry Demarest Lloyd launches "muckraking" journalism by blasting Standard Oil

1882
The Standard Oil Trust is formed

1884
Legally a New Yorker, buys a townhouse in Manhattan

1885
Big wells arise near Lima, Ohio, which will help Standard Oil become a leading producer of crude oil and natural gas

1889
Pledges the first $600,000 of what will eventually be $35 million to the University of Chicago

1890
Sherman Antitrust Act challenges monopolies such as Standard Oil's

1892
Standard Oil Trust dissolves, but Standard Oil continues to thrive

1901
Rockefeller Institute for Medical Research, today Rockefeller University, opens with the first installment of an eventual $61 million from its namesake

1902
Buys a golf club in Lakewood, New Jersey, to pursue his new hobby; Ida M. Tarbell launches the damaging *History of the Standard Oil Company*

1903
Forms the General Education Board with the first of $129 million

1911
The U.S. Supreme Court breaks up Standard

1913
Begins to endow the new Rockefeller Foundation with $183 million; his son and aides spark another deadly strike, this time by Colorado miners

1915
Laura Rockefeller dies

1919
Buys The Casements, a home in Ormond Beach, Florida

1937
Dies at The Casements

FURTHER READING AND RESOURCES

BOOKS ABOUT JOHN D. ROCKEFELLER AND HIS FAMILY

Chernow, Ron. *Titan: The Life of John D. Rockefeller, Sr.* New York: Random House, 1998.

Collier, Peter, and David Horowitz. *The Rockefellers: An American Dynasty.* New York: Holt, Rinehart and Winston, 1976.

Ernst, Joseph W., ed. *"Dear Father" / "Dear Son": Correspondence of John D. Rockefeller and John D. Rockefeller, Jr.* New York: Fordham University Press in cooperation with Rockefeller Archive Center, 1994.

Fosdick, Raymond B. *John D. Rockefeller, Jr.: A Portrait.* New York: Harper and Brothers, 1956.

Goulder, Grace. *John D. Rockefeller: The Cleveland Years.* Cleveland: Western Reserve Historical Society, 1972.

Harr, John Ensor, and Peter J. Johnson. *The Rockefeller Century.* New York: Charles Scribner's Sons, 1988.

Hawke, David Freeman. *John D.: The Founding Father of the Rockefellers.* New York: Harper and Row, 1980.

Josephson, Matthew. *The Robber Barons: The Great American Capitalists, 1861–1901.* 1934. Reprint, New York: Harcourt Brace, 1995.

Lloyd, Henry Demarest. *Wealth Against Commonwealth.* 1894. Reprint, Westport, Conn.: Greenwood, 1976.

Nevins, Allan. *John D. Rockefeller.* New York: Charles Scribner's Sons, 1959.

Rockefeller, John D. *Random Reminiscences of Men and Events.* 1909. Reprint, Tarrytown, N.Y.: Sleepy Hollow Press and Rockefeller Archive Center, 1984.

Stasz, Clarice. *The Rockefeller Women: Dynasty of Piety, Privacy, and Service.* New York: St. Martin's, 1995.

Tarbell, Ida M. *The History of the Standard Oil Company: Briefer Version.* David M. Chalmers, ed. New York: W.W. Norton, 1969.

Books about Rockefeller's Associates, Adversaries, Fields, or Era

Chandler, David Leon. *Henry Flagler: The Astonishing Life and Times of the Visionary Robber Baron Who Founded Florida.* New York: Macmillan, 1986.

Dolson, Hildegarde. *The Great Oildorado: The Gaudy and Turbulent Years of the First Oil Rush: Pennsylvania, 1859–1880.* New York: Random House, 1959.

Gleisser, Marcus. *The World of Cyrus Eaton.* New York: A.S. Barnes, 1965.

Greenwood, Janette Thomas. *The Gilded Age: A History in Documents.* New York: Oxford University Press, 2000.

Henderson, Wayne, and Scott Benjamin. *Standard Oil: The First 125 Years.* Osceola, Wis.: Motorbooks International, 1996.

Hofstadter, Richard. *The Age of Reform: From Bryan to F.D.R.* New York: Knopf, 1989.

Leuzzi, Linda. *Life in America 100 Years Ago: Industry and Business.* Philadelphia: Chelsea House, 1997.

Meltzer, Milton. *The Many Lives of Andrew Carnegie.* New York: Franklin Watts, 1997.

———. *Theodore Roosevelt and His America.* New York: Franklin Watts, 1994.

O'Toole, Thomas. *The Economic History of the United States.* Minneapolis, Minn.: Lerner, 1990.

Roosevelt, Theodore. *Theodore Roosevelt: An Autobiography.* New York: Charles Scribner's Sons, 1925.

Yergin, Daniel. *The Prize: The Epic Quest for Oil, Money, and Power.* New York: Simon & Schuster, 1991.

Organizations

The following organizations do not accept drop-in visitors but may be contacted for information:

Rockefeller Archive Center, 15 Dayton Avenue, North Tarrytown, NY 10591–1598. www.rockefeller.edu/archive.ctr

Rockefeller Foundation, 420 Fifth Avenue, New York, NY 10018. www.rockfound.org

Rockefeller University, Office of Public Affairs, 1230 York Avenue, New York, NY 10021. www.rockefeller.edu

Museums and Historic Sites

Brooklyn Museum

200 Eastern Parkway
Brooklyn, NY 11238
Telephone: 718-638-5000
www.brooklynart.org

Contains one room from Rockefeller's townhouse.

The Casements

25 Riverside Drive
Ormond Beach, FL 32176
Telephone: 904-676-3216

Rockefeller's former winter home, now a cultural and civic center.

Drake Well Museum

East Bloss Street Extension
Rural Delivery 3
P.O. Box 7
Titusville, PA 16354
Telephone: 814-827-2797
www.drakewell.org

Oil memorabilia, including a working replica of an early well.

Henry Morrison Flagler Museum (Whitehall)

1 Whitehall Way
P.O. Box 969
Palm Beach, FL 33480
Telephone: 561-655-2833
www.flagler.org

Former home of Rockefeller's partner.

Kykuit House

Pocantico Hills, New York
Reservations or information:
Historic Hudson Valley
150 White Plains Road
Tarrytown, NY 10591
Telephone: 914-631-9491
www.hudsonvalley.org

Former home of John D. Rockefeller and descendants. Contains leading works of 20th-century art.

Museum of American Financial History

28 Broadway
New York, NY 10004-1763
Telephone: 212-908-4110
www.financialhistory.org

Contains Rockefeller strongbox and documents and memorabilia about business in his era.

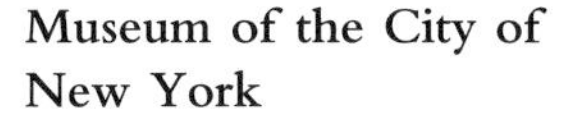

Museum of the City of New York

1220 Fifth Avenue
New York, NY 10029
Telephone: 212-534-1672
www.mcny.org

Contains two rooms from Rockefeller's Manhattan townhouse.

Rockefeller Center

Centered at
30 Rockefeller Plaza
New York, NY 10112
Telephone: 212-332-6868

World's biggest privately owned complex for entertainment and business.

Union Church of Pocantico Hills

555 Bedford Road
Pocantico Hills, NY
Visitor information:
Historic Hudson Valley
150 White Plains Road
Tarrytown, NY 10591
Telephone: 914-631-8200
www.hudsonvalley.org

Features stained glass windows by Marc Chagall and Henri Matisse, commissioned by members of Rockefeller's family in memory of John Jr. and Abby Aldrich, respectively.

University of Chicago

5801 South Ellis Avenue
Chicago, IL 60637
Telephone: 773-702-1234
www.uchicago.edu

School founded largely by Rockefeller.

Western Reserve Historical Society

10825 East Boulevard
Cleveland, OH 44106
Telephone: 216-721-5722
www.wrhs.org

Contains Rockefeller letters, Standard Oil memorabilia, and materials about Cleveland in Rockefeller's day.

INDEX

References to illustrations and their captions are indicated by page numbers in *italic*.

ACKNOWLEDGMENTS

I wish to thank the Rockefeller Archive Center for its generous research, guidance, and permission for quotations. The archive is part of Rockefeller University, which gave me additional information and hospitality at its main campus. In Cleveland, the Cleveland Public Library and Lake View Cemetery provided many hours of help. My further thanks to Historic Hudson Valley, Rockefeller Foundation, Western Reserve Historical Society, British Petroleum, David N. Myers College, Cuyahoga County Archives, Museum of the City of New York, American Museum of Financial History, Bridgeport (Conn.) Public Library, Oakland Cemetery (Freeport, Ill.), Ted Schwarz, Dr. Neal Chandler, Dr. Allan Peskin, Wayne Henderson, Scott Benjamin, W. Clark Miller, Koeppel and Koeppel Real Estate Company, David Rockefeller, and Mr. Rockefeller's associate, Peter J. Johnson. Finally, many thanks to my editor, Nancy Toff, for publishing my first book.

Picture Credits

Corbis-Bettmann: 40; Gary Tong: 115; Library of Congress, Prints & Photographs Division: 62 (LC-USZ62-11319), 86 (LC-USZ62-61409), 95 (LC-USZ62-26205); Museum of American Financial History: 28, 50, 56, 76, 101; New York Public Library: 60; From Pennsylvania Historical & Museum Commission, Drake Well Museum Collection, Titusville, Penn.: 29; The Plain Dealer: 81; Courtesy of the Rockefeller Archive Center: 2, 8, 11, 12, 17, 22, 27, 34, 37, 43, 52, 53, 64, 71, 72, 75, 83, 92, 98, 108, 110, 111, 114; The University of Chicago Library, Department of Special Collections: cover.

Text Credits

Thankful, Thankful, Thankful, p. 33: Courtesy Rockefeller Archive Center, North Tarrytown, NY.

Almost an Unfriendly Disposition, p. 45: Courtesy Rockefeller Archive Center, North Tarrytown, NY.

High-Class Dealing, p. 97: John D. Rockefeller, *Random Reminiscences of Men and Events.* New York: Doubleday, Page, 1909, 132–3.

What a Providence!, p. 113: Courtesy Rockefeller Archive Center, North Tarrytown, NY.

Grant Segall is a general assignment and feature reporter for the Cleveland *Plain Dealer.* He has also published fiction in university journals and freelanced for *The Washington Post, Time,* and many other publications. Segall was born and raised in greater New York, near two of John D. Rockefeller's homes. He later lived on the former grounds of a third outside Cleveland. Now he lives in nearby Shaker Heights, with his wife, Victoria Belfiglio, and their three children, David, Anthony, and Mario.